Praise for *Get Scrappy*

"Nick shows us why money is the bane of creativity. No budget? No problem. This useful and entertaining book shows us how to put brains before budget."

— Mark W. Schaefer, Schaefer Marketing Solutions,
author of *The Content Code*

"While every other book out there gets more complex, this one gives you a whole lot of simple, common-sense practices to take your business to the next level. This book will just plain work for you."

— Joe Pulizzi, Founder, Content Marketing Institute
and author of *Content Inc.*

"*Get Scrappy* provides a marketing roadmap anyone can use . . . big, small, non-profit, corporate . . . and couldn't we all work a little smarter?"

— Carie Lewis Carlson, Director, Communications Marketing,
The Humane Society of the United States

"If marketing your business seems like a Herculean task, don't worry! Just *Get Scrappy* and dig into Nick Westergaard's book."

— Michael Stelzner, author of *Launch*
and Founder of Social Media Examiner

"The modern era of marketing feels like what would happen if you gave every fifteen-year-old the keys to their own car without bothering to teach them how to drive. Some would be fine, others would crash, and the rest would never even get the engine started. Nick Westergaard's new book is like modern marketing Driver's Ed, if Driver's Ed were really smart, funny, and surprising. After reading *Get Scrappy*, I think I'm finally ready to leave my driveway."

— Heidi Grant Halvorson, Ph.D., best-selling author of *Nine Things Successful People Do Differently* and *No One Understands You and What to Do About It*

"Want to get better at digital marketing? Read this book. In it, Nick successfully argues that to win in the age of 'Ooh, shiny!' one needs to be smarter, faster, and come up with better ideas. *Get Scrappy* will help you do that."

— Pete Shankman, author of *Zombie Loyalists: Using Great Service to Create Rabid Fans*

"The whole of Westergaard's book is important, but Part Three will hone you down into a sharp and useful instrument of magic. This book delivers!"

— Chris Brogan, CEO Owner Media Group and coauthor
of the *New York Times* best-seller *Trust Agents*

"In the age of the customer you have to know more than just the buzzwords, trends, and technology. Nick helps you become a scrappy marketer so you can build strong relationships with your customers and engage them in your community."

— Mike Gerholdt, Admin Evangelist at Salesforce
and host of the ButtonClick Admin podcast

"I wish more brands would get scrappy with their marketing. Digital marketing used to be a panacea because it was fast, cheap and data-driven. Now, too many brands see marketing as slow, expensive, and filled with so much data that they are paralyzed by it. Big mistake. Get scrappy. It's not just the name of this great book by Nick Westergaard, it's an attitude that all brands need to embrace, strategize and execute on. Here's your roadmap."

— Mitch Joel, President, Mirum, author of
Six Pixels of Separation and *CTRL ALT Delete*

"As the owner of a small business with an expanding brand, I will genuinely recommend *Get Scrappy* to friends and colleagues, both seasoned professionals and those new to the challenges of business marketing, as it is a must-read for anyone looking to broaden their reach with limited resources! *Get Scrappy* not only gives you the logical steps you need to be successful, it offers tools and thought-provoking questions that just will change how you think about your brand!"

— Natalie Brown, Owner, Scratch Cupcakery

"Big budgets don't guarantee success and scrappiness isn't unique to small companies. Having worked at a large company that knew how to be scrappy, I can tell you that we practiced the principles that Nick so adeptly lays out. Using these techniques, regardless of budget, will change your results."

— Scott Monty, Principal and Founder,
Scott Monty Strategies

"Technology is changing the way marketers approach their jobs more quickly than ever before. Thought you couldn't keep up last year? Welcome to another new year that will introduce dozens of new technologies, social media networks, and more content ideas than you could ever possibly produce. With all of that comes a need for resources—both time and money: both things most of us don't have (that is, until I figure out a way to duplicate time). Combine all of that with the shiny new object, the myth of big, and the checklist marketing and we're suddenly faced with a future of insanity. But it doesn't have to be that way! In *Get Scrappy* Nick Westergaard presents a marketing system any organization and any marketer can use: anyone who could use a few people and a few dollars more. It doesn't mean you have to think small. It means you have to roll up your sleeves, be creative, and get scrappy. Now 'doing more with less' won't grate on your nerves because you'll have figured out how to do exactly that. So get to it!"

— Gini Dietrich, CEO of Arment Dietrich and author of *Spin Sucks*

"*Get Scrappy* has never been more important, or more realistic, marketing advice than it is today. Technology has leveled the playing field and any business of any size can compete with a scrappy attitude. This book will help you get there."

— Jim Tobin, author of *Social Media Is a Cocktail Party* and *Earn It. Don't Buy It.*

"The flaw with most marketing advice you get from speakers and bloggers and authors is that it's dependent on having a big team, a big budget and resources the big brands are used to dealing with. Nick Westergaard has filled the gap in the advice out there with this book. Everyone from a small business owner just starting to a big corporation CMO can follow this book and build the basic framework of a successful marketing effort. Roll up your sleeves. You're about to learn how to get scrappy."

— Jason Falls, coauthor of *No Bullshit Social Media: The All-Business, No-Hype Guide to Social Media Marketing*, and Senior Vice President, Elasticity

"*Get Scrappy* is your guidebook to mastering digital marketing no matter the size of your business or the industry it operates in. *Get Scrappy* shows you how to be smarter in your business as well as more effective and efficient in your marketing efforts. If you listen to Nick and follow his advice, he'll help you take your business to the next level!"

— Mack Collier, digital marketing strategist and author of *Think Like a Rock Star: How to Create Social Media and Marketing Strategies That Turn Customers into Fans*

"If you want to do more with less (and who doesn't?!), Nick Westergaard's book is the ultimate guide to marketing. Read it to learn an immensely practical and creative system for addressing age-old marketing challenges as well as seizing the new opportunities of social and digital today."

— Denise Lee Yohn, brand-building expert, speaker, and author of *What Great Brands Do*

"When it comes to marketing your business in the digital age, so much of what you read in books these days is theory-based thoughts on where business is headed, but oftentimes these same books are not practical enough to truly apply to your business. But in *Get Scrappy*, Nick Westergaard has truly come through with a work that, if applied, will absolutely have a powerful impact on not just your business, but your bottom line as well. Even better, the techniques and principles taught therein apply across the board, be it big or small business, B2B or B2C—this is a book that has the word "application" written all over it. Well done, Nick Westergaard, well done."

—Marcus Sheridan, professional speaker, Founder of The Sales Lion, Partner at River Pools and Spas

GET
SCRAPPY

$$- \ - \ - \ - \ - \ - \ - \ - \ - \ -$$

Smarter Digital Marketing for Businesses Big and Small

NICK WESTERGAARD

AMACOM

AMERICAN MANAGEMENT ASSOCIATION

New York · Atlanta · Brussels · Chicago · Mexico City
San Francisco · Shanghai · Tokyo · Toronto · Washington, D.C.

Bulk discounts available. For details visit:
www.amacombooks.org/go/specialsales
Or contact special sales:
Phone: 800-250-5308
Email: specialsls@amanet.org
View all the AMACOM titles at: www.amacombooks.org
American Management Association: www.amanet.org

Library of Congress Cataloging-in-Publication Data

Names: Westergaard, Nick, author.
Title: Get scrappy : smarter digital marketing for businesses big and small / Nick Westergaard.
Description: New York : American Management Association, [2016] | Includes bibliographical references and index.
Identifiers: LCCN 2015045508 (print) | LCCN 2015047287 (ebook) | ISBN 9780814437315 (hardcover) | ISBN 9780814437322 (ebook)
Subjects: LCSH: Internet marketing. | Internet advertising. | Digital media. | Marketing — Management.
Classification: LCC HF5415.1265 .W473 2016 (print) | LCC HF5415.1265 (ebook) | DDC 658.8/72—dc23
LC record available at http://lccn.loc.gov/2015045508

About AMA

American Management Association (www.amanet.org) is a world leader in talent development, advancing the skills of individuals to drive business success. Our mission is to support the goals of individuals and organizations through a complete range of products and services, including classroom and virtual seminars, webcasts, webinars, podcasts, conferences, corporate and government solutions, business books, and research. AMA's approach to improving performance combines experiential learning—learning through doing—with opportunities for ongoing professional growth at every step of one's career journey.

Printing number
10 9 8 7 6 5 4 3 2 1

For Harry, Sam, Adrien, Mia, and Jude,
the small people in my life who inspire big things.

And for Meghann, the scrappiest person I know.

CONTENTS

Appendix

FOREWORD

My favorite example of scrappy marketing comes from the Humane Society of Silicon Valley in Millbrae, California.

Just before Christmas of 2014, the shelter had taken in a little jerk of a dog—a Chihuahua named "Eddie the Terrible."

Eddie was a handful. He snapped at other dogs. He didn't like kids. He was socially awkward. And he had very specific sleeping demands—as in: as close to a human being as he could possibly press his small, yellow body.

So what does a shelter do with a dog like that? A dog that is anything but low-maintenance? A dog that will never pull Timmy out of the well, as Finnegan Dowling, the shelter's social media manager, put it?

In Eddie's case, the shelter simply leaned into the kind of marketing Nick Westergaard describes in this book.

Rather than talking up Eddie's merits, the shelter actively *discouraged* people from adopting him. They underscored his shortcomings in a series of graphics and blog posts. They wrote a ridiculously creative, hilarious, and honest adoption listing for him.

- - -

"We're not expecting you to want to meet him, but if you must we really can't deter you," they wrote in the post about Eddie titled "Three Reasons You Don't Want to Adopt Eddie the Terrible." In other words, they pivoted completely from the typical shelter pet marketing efforts. And in doing so they told a different kind of story about Eddie—one refreshingly and unusually honest, and one that ironically made complex little Eddie (and all of his problems) all the more endearing.

That scrappy approach made Eddie's story go viral. (And, happily, Eddie found a home for the holidays with a sufficiently antisocial couple. No kids.)

I love the story of Eddie. But I also love that a nonprofit with a minuscule marketing budget was able to do so much with so little, just by thinking scrappy.

The shelter's creativity with Eddie's story, perseverance in the face of what most would have considered an untenable situation, and heart to do what was best for the tiny terror of a dog embodies the scrappy marketing mindset.

We all can do the same. We all can adopt a mindset that helps us make the most of what we have—and turn limited resources into an advantage.

Because, in my experience, marketers are always strapped for cash. That's true of the marketing leaders in the world's largest corporations. And it's true of pet shelters and other nonprofits, too. No one ever thinks they have enough resources, budget, or ability to consistently create truly great marketing.

But, guess what? You absolutely do.

You just need to know where to look. And, lucky for you, you're now holding in your hands the very book that will tell you exactly that.

Nick's book is a great blueprint for any business looking to work smarter with the resources at hand. He gives you the tools you need to both concentrate and simplify your marketing efforts, and to make sense of this complex marketing world we live in.

With engaging examples and real-world advice, Nick shows you how a little creativity, planning, and strategic elbow grease will help you grow your business. And he tells you how you focus your efforts to get real results. Even if, by the way, your "product" isn't a terrible but misunderstood little dog named Eddie!

Ready? Let's get scrappy!

Ann Handley

Chief Content Officer, MarketingProfs

Author of the *Wall Street Journal* best-seller, *Everybody Writes* (2014)

www.annhandley.com

INTRODUCTION

scrappy, *adjective*. *Describing someone or something that appears dwarfed by a challenge, but more than compensates for seeming inadequacies through will, persistence, and heart.*

(Urban Dictionary)

"Do I really need another marketing book?"

This was probably going through your head when you saw this book. Our shelves are bursting at the seams with marketing books for one simple reason: This is an exciting time to be in marketing. The Internet, social media, and content marketing have forever changed the way we build brands and market our organizations. These shifts have reset the playing field to the advantage of businesses big and small.

And yet, it's also a frustrating time to be in marketing, as we struggle to keep up and overcome obstacles. While many understand the potential unleashed by these digital shifts, few are truly prepared for it. The Internet has changed how we plan, staff, manage, and measure our marketing. There's a lot of work that needs to be done and, for many businesses, resources are minimal. We understand the *why* behind these marketing shifts. What many marketers struggle with is the *how*. *How will all of this get done in a meaningful manner with the resources we have?* This book is for the marketers who want to get stuff done.

As a brand strategist, keynote speaker, and college educator, I help thousands of marketers every year. From small businesses to the Fortune 500 to the President's Jobs Council. From seasoned marketing pros to marketing students. From the plains of the Midwest to cities in Europe. And they all struggle with the same challenges—the same ones you are facing.

To paraphrase Charles Dickens, it is the best of times, it is the worst of times. Dickens wasn't talking about marketing today, but he could have been. For marketers, this is the best of times. Technology has enabled new forms of media such as Facebook and Twitter, which allow us to reach more people, more economically and easily than ever before. We can build direct, personal relationships with our customers. We can help, inform, entertain, interact, and instruct. And as a result, we can create enormous value on our own powerful platforms and channels.

Now we come to the worst of times. While we face many challenges, there are three main obstacles that stand in our way.

1. **Shiny New Things.** We're distracted by all of the shiny new things online: new channels, features, platforms, and networks are constantly coming at us. *Ooh! Shiny! What's your brand doing on Snapchat? How about that new Instagram feature? Or that awesome new platform that integrates all of your social media activity and makes you breakfast while it does all of this?* Okay, so the last one isn't here (yet!) but you get the idea.

2. The Myth of Big. Budgets are tighter than ever. Only big brands with big budgets, big teams, and big technology can do big things with digital marketing today, or so it feels sometimes. Dwarfed by this imagined competition, many end up collapsing into self-pity as they sigh, "That's cool but we couldn't do that here."

3. Checklist Marketing. This is when we focus on checking things off lists instead of on what makes the most sense. For fear of ending up in the boss's crosshairs because he saw a story about Facebook advertising on CNBC, many marketers take a checklist approach. Facebook? Check. Twitter? Check. LinkedIn group? Yep. Instagram? We got that, too. Is any of this working?! Awkward silence.

Marketers have more opportunities than ever before. How do we capitalize on this unprecedented time in marketing history while maintaining our budgets and our sanity?

GET SCRAPPY

As you approach your marketing, don't get frustrated. Get scrappy instead. At this point, you may be asking, "What is scrappy?" Let's start with what scrappy isn't. Scrappy isn't marketing small. Scrappy isn't marketing on the cheap. And, most importantly, scrappy isn't dumbing down your marketing.

Merriam-Webster Collegiate defines *scrappy* as having an aggressive or determined spirit.[1] My favorite definition comes from the Urban Dictionary, which defines *scrappy* as describing "someone or something that appears dwarfed by a challenge, but more than compensates for seeming inadequacies through will, persistence, and heart."[2]

Ultimately, the size of your organization doesn't matter. Business-to-business vs. business-to-consumer, nonprofit vs. for-profit doesn't either. The local dry cleaner who does its own marketing can benefit from getting scrappy just as much as a marketer in a larger organization. As Samantha Hersil, who leads digital marketing at Pacific Cycle for brands like Schwinn, Kid Trax, and Roadmaster, told me, "We all wish that we had a few people and a few dollars more."[3]

Regardless of how different our organizations and brands may be, we all face the same hurdles that can be overcome with will, persistence, and heart—tapping into that feistiness and edge of getting scrappy. Scrappy is doing more with less. Scrappy is a spirit determined to simplify marketing in today's complex digital world.

Scrappy is thinking like an underdog (even if you aren't) with a winning and determined mindset. Let's explore that mindset a little further.

THE SCRAPPY MINDSET

If scrappiness is a state of mind that can be useful to anyone at any organization large or small, what does it entail? And, more importantly, how can you harness the power of scrappy to help you do more with less? To better understand how you can get scrappy with your marketing, let's explore the three core attributes that make up the Scrappy Mindset.

Brains Before Budget—Whether you are a marketing director at a Fortune 500 company, a nonprofit development director, or a one-person marketing department at a small business, we're all susceptible to the monetary implications of the Myth of Big. When you start to think about personnel, tools, and technology, digital marketing can get real expensive real fast.

Remember, getting scrappy is more than just being cheap. Scrappy also isn't about dumbing down your marketing and saving your brain cells. In fact, getting scrappy is about using more of your brain to help you do more with less. That's why a key tenet of the Scrappy Mindset is putting your brains before your budget. To do more with less, you need to first define what it is that you're doing.

All of this thinking doesn't stop once your marketing strategy is approved either. You need to continue to look for smarter ways around the challenges you face. When you get scrappy, you start to see the value that you can harness from your internal team, your community of customers, and other unexpected sources.

Market Like a Mousetrap — As the famous saying often credited to Ralph Waldo Emerson goes, "Build a better mousetrap, and the world will beat a path to your door." And yet, despite the fact that inventors each year for nearly a century have gotten patents for supposedly improved versions, these paths remain unbeaten as nothing has proved more useful than the simple spring-loaded bar mousetrap invented by William C. Hooker of Abingdon, Illinois.[4] That's because the mousetrap is both effective and efficient.

My family lives in a rambling old house. It's the kind of house that has character. It's also the kind of house that mice love when it cools off in the fall. While working in my home office, I occasionally hear little squeaks and scratches inside my walls. However, there's no cause for alarm as I've set several Victor mousetraps throughout the house. If there's a mouse, it won't be around for long. *The mousetrap is effective.* And you can't beat the price. At most stores, a couple dollars buys you a pack of two traps or more. *The mousetrap is efficient.*

Like the mousetrap, to get scrappy with your marketing, you have to be both effective and efficient. To be effective, your objective has to be clearly defined first (the trap's objective is pretty obvious) so that you know when the job is done (*snap!*). Efficiency provides the best construct for a more scrappy relationship with money. Being efficient is more than just being cheap. You've still met your desired objective. You've just done so with minimal expense.

See Ideas Everywhere— Jeremy Gutsche, innovation expert, best-selling author, and CEO of Trend Hunter, says that we're currently in a period of history's highest rate of change. "It's not just the new things. It's the pace of change."[5] That's why marketers often turn to case studies to help make sense of this ever-changing world. While case studies can be useful, sometimes we focus so intently on how different our own business is that we miss out on valuable insights from unexpected sources.

Stay open to ideas from outside your industry. *Nope. That's a B2C idea. We're B2B. That won't work here.* Or perhaps, *That's too business-y. We're a nonprofit and things are sooooooo different for us.* Many times you can have an even greater impact because it's an approach that's not often taken in your industry. Cloud-computing giant Salesforce developed an app that allowed fans to create custom Valentine's Day e-cards to share via social media. *Wait! Isn't Valentine's Day a consumer-focused holiday? Isn't Salesforce a B2B company?* Maybe, but they had some fun and stood out in a big way by daring to think beyond their own sector stereotypes.

Technology is moving too fast for you to be confined by the proven ideas in your industry. To stay ahead, you have to learn to collect insights and ideas from beyond your specific niche and industry. In the heyday of the direct mail era, marketers kept physical files of mailers they liked for future ideas they could "swipe." The scrappy marketer knows to keep a digital swipe file (trade the file folder for Google Docs or Evernote) for useful ideas from a variety of sources. Disclosure: Not every case study shared in this book is from a business just like yours. But I promise you there's something you can learn from each and every example. If you need some encouragement, think of *Saturday Night Live*'s Stuart Smalley: "You're good enough, you're smart enough, and doggone it, you can steal this marketing idea and make it work for you." Okay, so I adapted that last part a bit but I was just making something from another industry work for me.

To get scrappy you need to remember to (1) put your brains before your budget, (2) market like a mousetrap, and (3) see ideas everywhere. Then and only then can you start doing more with less. More isn't always better. Sometimes it's just more. By embracing this mindset, you can get scrappy with your marketing as others are already doing—at organizations big and small.

- - - - - - - - - - - - - - - -
SUPER BOWL TO SEWER MAN: SCRAPPY MARKETERS ARE EVERYWHERE

You don't have to look far to find marketers getting scrappy.

Each year brands shell out millions to be a part of the Super Bowl. The going rate for a 30-second ad slot during the game at the time of writing is $4.5 million.[6] In recent years, social media has provided viewers and marketers alike with a new experience on their second screen, following and engaging in social media conversations around hashtags such as #SuperBowlAds and #brandbowl. This online activity has led brands to maximize their investment and exposure by releasing their ads in the week leading up to the big game.

Newcastle Brown Ale took advantage of this online opportunity to get scrappy during Super Bowl XLVIII. Because it's owned by

Heineken, you might not think of Newcastle as a scrappy underdog. When compared with the rest of the beer category in the U.S.,
however, the U.K. workingman's ale is dwarfed by giants such as
Anheuser-Busch and MillerCoors. With Budweiser as the official
beer of the Super Bowl, Anheuser-Busch reserved 3.5 minutes of air
time in 2014, easily costing $30 million.[7]
And yet, Newcastle scored big points for a fraction of the cost.
How? By releasing a YouTube video among the other leaked Super
Bowl ads featuring *Pitch Perfect* star Anna Kendrick gossiping about
Newcastle's "megahuge Super Bowl ad that didn't get made." The
non-ad was set to star Kendrick, who confesses to being "hot but not
'beer commercial babe' hot" in a hilarious two-minute send-up of
celebrity culture and the inflated stakes around Super Bowl ads. The
video closes with the hashtag #IfWeMadeIt, which set up Newcastle's digital strategy during the game itself.

While the Kendrick video never aired, it gained 4 million views
on YouTube in a week and was considered a "Super Bowl ad" by
many people. During the game, Newcastle tweeted to each brand
that advertised, complimenting their ad while linking to YouTube
parodies for each ad sketched out in a simple, hand-drawn story-
board format with a narrator pitching the ad #IfWeMadeIt (you
tube.com/newcastle).

Scrappy marketing can work for businesses of all shapes and
sizes. My wife and I have five kids. Amidst our controlled craziness,
we need all of our toilets up and running at all times to prevent any
number of domestic disasters. Recently, we had a two-toilet emer-
gency and called Hawkeye Sewer and Drain to come bail us out.
After the job, as I was paying the plumber and walking him out of
our house, he stopped and asked me, "Do you have a copy of our
latest newsletter?" I did not. (Why would I?) Then he handed me a
copy of Sewer Science, an informative newsletter printed on bright

gold paper featuring engaging articles such as "Is Your Toilet Paper the Problem? How Can You Know?"

Falling into the trap of Checklist Marketing, it would have been easy for the Sewer Man (owner Jeff Waite's self-applied nickname) to invest tons of money to develop a cool mobile app or direct customers to the latest, greatest social media channel. While the articles in his newsletter all live online as well, he took a chance on producing highly valuable content (seriously—you should read the articles) delivered in print at an incredibly relevant moment. Think about it. Once your problem is fixed and the plumber is out the door, your interest in plumbing wanes considerably.

Marketing snobs could dismiss this as an old-school tactic. However, the strategy behind Sewer Science isn't just spot on. It's scrappy. Like Newcastle, the Sewer Man put his brains before his budget and created marketing that was both effective and efficient like the mousetrap.

Marketers of all shapes and sizes can do more with less by getting scrappy. What are you waiting for?

YOUR GUIDE TO SMARTER DIGITAL MARKETING

Remember all of those marketing books I mentioned earlier? Too many examine the *why* behind these shifts without focusing on the *how*.

Confession: My name is Nick and I'm a book addict. My office is packed full of bookcases and book stacks. However, there's one characteristic that unites the books that sit closest to my desk: All are ragged, dog-eared, and chock-full of notes. In picking them up you may find a broken spine where the book flops open to a certain page or a cover that's on the verge of falling off.

That's because these books serve as consistent reference points in my day-to-day life as a marketer. The best business books not only teach you a philosophy for thinking about your work, they also arm you with tools and systems to go forth and do that work. My goal with *Get Scrappy* is to create a valuable resource for you. I hope you break the spine, dog-ear the pages, and write in the margins. Like you would with a valuable handbook or trusty guide.

The challenges you face as a marketer are both strategic and tactical. Both big picture and boots on the ground. You need guiding philosophies as well as practical how-tos. That's why I've organized this book into three parts. Scrappy marketers look before they leap. Part One focuses on the smart steps that you can't skip if you want to properly ground your marketing. Having a solid strategy is the only way to see past all of the Shiny New Things in our complex digital world. Part Two is about doing the work—specifically, how you can do more with less and overcome the Myth of Big.

Finally, in Part Three, it's time to measure, manage, and, most importantly, simplify—making your efforts leaner, meaner, and more effective and efficient for the long haul. Then and only then can you avoid Checklist Marketing and target your precious resources on what matters most. Throughout this process, you'll need to remember the value in seeing ideas everywhere, identifying the ideas you can potentially adapt from outside your industry.

As this book aims to be practical and tactical, each chapter will conclude with "Next Steps" prompts to help you start applying these concepts in your marketing. Remember, I want you to make notes in the book. A useful handbook should look a little banged up and scribbled in. At the end, you'll also find an appendix featuring a handy reference guide or "scrappy summary," a list for further reading, and discussion questions for helping you share these ideas with your coworkers, classroom, or reading group.

Get Scrappy will help you:

- Demystify digital marketing today in a way that makes sense for your business.

- Ground your marketing with strategy that lays a foundation for action.

- Build a strong brand with something to say.

- Employ social media and content as a part of your brand's marketing mix.

- Integrate digital and non-digital marketing touch points in a meaningful way.

The result is a reliable, repeatable system for reinventing your marketing as marketing reinvents itself.

Now, are you ready to get scrappy? Let's get started.

Part One

SMART STEPS YOU CAN'T SKIP

Chapter 1

THE BRAND BEHIND
THE MEGAPHONE

Is digital marketing really that complex? Just start a Facebook page. Publish a blog. Record a podcast. Share photos on Instagram. What's the big deal? We can do all of that in about an hour? Why are we making a fuss about how hard all of this is?

That's the siren call of Shiny New Things. Sure, it's easier than ever to start. The tools and technologies that can help you be a better marketer are deceptively simple to employ. However, when you take a step back and consider the Scrappy Mindset—putting brains before budget, marketing like a mousetrap, and seeing ideas everywhere—you know that you can do better. You have to do better.

That's why the first step in getting scrappy is getting smart. Putting strategy first and ensuring that you know what it is you're trying to do in the first place. This not only leads to better marketing out of the gate, it also helps you measure what matters so that you can optimize your work for the long haul.

Sounds pretty logical, right? And yet, too many marketers are quick to rush in and start marketing without a plan in place. That's why we're beginning our journey with three critical smart steps you can't skip. Here in Chapter 1, you'll discover that although marketing has changed significantly in recent years, what's behind it has not. The tactics may have changed but the underlying strategy remains. You still need to build a strong brand with something to say. This is easier said than done. Along the way, we'll unpack a simple five-step blueprint you can use to help you define your brand.

In Chapter 2, you'll throw stuffy strategies out the window and instead map a path to marketing success. With a brand packed up and a journey plotted, you can start selecting the social media and digital marketing tools that will take you to your destination. Once again, Shiny New Things distract. That's why you'll need the digital compass presented in Chapter 3. This compass will help you find your way and determine what digital channels work best when.

As you build a smart, scrappy foundation, you need some context to understand how we got here.

THE CHANGING MARKETING MEGAPHONE

Why is marketing so different today? As astrophysicist Neil deGrasse Tyson says in explaining a simple little topic like the universe, "Knowing where you came from is no less important than knowing where you're going."[1] Marketing has always been a tool for helping people and organizations share their wares with the hopes of producing profitable exchanges. Marketing communication has essentially been a megaphone for gaining attention.

But that marketing megaphone has changed a bit over the past several centuries. You could say that new media was born in Germany in the 1400s when Gutenberg revolutionized printing technology, enabling the first form of mass communication. And for the next 400 years, marketing was driven by print, from posters and newspapers to magazines and catalogs. There probably weren't as many books about navigating media shifts as several centuries passed *without* any major shifts!

It wasn't until the early 20th century that we had our senses of sound and sight awoken by radio, television, and the birth of broadcast media. This new media shift had an easy-to-understand dynamic. As there were only a few ways to reach the masses, more radio and TV ads sold more products and got companies more shelf space, which they could use to buy even more ads. Bigger was better, making this the birth of the Myth of Big as well. Only big brands with big budgets could do truly big things.

While we didn't go hundreds of years before the next media shift, broadcast advertising ruled most of the 20th century. In addition to bringing us Nirvana and *90210*, the '90s also brought the first widespread use of the Internet. And with it, the most rapidly evolving form of media. From email marketing (still a formidable force which we'll discuss later in the book) to this past decade's Facebook, Instagram, and Snapchat, each new digital innovation has quickly found its way onto the radars of marketers.

It's easy to look at this timeline and think only of the rapid rate of change—the chaos that has disrupted the slow and steady climb of traditional, bigger-is-better media. However, we can't lose sight of the baseline. The common denominator. All of these tools help us build better brands. Now we have even more tools to do this. But to fully leverage this new marketing megaphone we first have to ensure that there's something behind it.

We have to take a look at the brand behind the megaphone.

DO WE REALLY HAVE TO TALK ABOUT BRANDING?

Branding? Really?? Yes, really.

Like the Amy Poehler and Seth Meyers Weekend Update bit

from *Saturday Night Live*, we *really* do have to talk about branding. (I said these were steps you can't skip.) Some roll their eyes at the very mention of branding. To some it's a dated construct. For others it's esoteric, touchy-feely homework that seems disconnected from bottom-line impact. Marketers may even view branding as yet another obstacle standing in the way as they launch their new digital efforts.

Even in today's fragmented culture, brands still matter. We're constantly reminded of the climbing user rates on social networks like Facebook and Twitter, yet another metric often falls through the cracks—something called "brand-following behavior," a measure of the rate at which individuals follow brands on social networks. In recent years, along with increases in engagement on social networks, brand-following behavior has doubled according to The Social Habit study conducted by Edison Research.[2] In their more comprehensive Infinite Dial study, Edison and partner Triton Digital found that one third of Americans age 12 and up knowingly follow brands on social media.[3]

Combine this with the fact that people by and large enjoy interacting on social media, and the opportunity for brands is clear. (When was the last time data reported high engagement levels with billboards and press releases? Has your brand-following behavior doubled for print ads?)

If you need further proof, The Social Habit also shows that even among a large national sample, when asked "which brand stands out on social media," we see it's a list of the usual suspects: Nike, Apple, Starbucks. At a glance, you could think that this just confirms the Myth of Big. A closer look reveals that these mega brands with millions of dollars and several decades of marketing muscle behind them all only rank in the single digits.

What does this mean for us? It means that these new forms of digital media have the potential to be a great brand equalizer.

Scrappy marketers might not expect to fare well on a poll of who's the most dominant TV advertiser, but new media levels the playing field in ways that we've never seen in the history of marketing.

It's only fitting that Lee Clow, the adman responsible for some of broadcast media's most prolific work, including Apple's 1984 and iconic iPod ads, would issue the best caution to marketers too quick to jump into the next big thing without first defining their brand. "The reality of the new media world is that if your brand does not have a belief, if it does not have a soul and does not correctly architect its messages everywhere it touches consumers, it can become irrelevant. It can be ignored, or even become a focal point for online contempt."[4] In short, you have to *be* something before you can *build* something.

The marketing megaphone may have changed, but making sure there's something behind it matters more than ever. That's why the critical first step in getting scrappy with your marketing is making sure your brand is clearly defined. As long as we're defining things, let's consider the definition of a brand.

SO, WHAT IS A BRAND?

Any good semantic exploration should start in a dictionary with a basic understanding of the word. Surprisingly, in a number of dictionaries our modern business-focused definition has overtaken the word's earliest meaning, which, according to the *Oxford English Dictionary* is "a piece of wood that is or has been burning on a hearth."[5] The *American Heritage Dictionary* shows as its first (not earliest) definition: "A trademark or distinctive name identifying a product, service, or organization."[6] This sense is also first in the *Random House Unabridged* (dictionary.reference.com).

Not a bad definition, but instead of relying on a dictionary, let's use the definition I employ when working with clients and speaking with businesses big and small:

> A brand can be any noun (person, place, or thing) that needs another party to take action (purchase, promote, advocate, and so on). A brand does this by creating a series of ideas and touch points that build a larger message which draws the desired audience close, engages them emotionally, and inspires them to take action.

Any brand can get scrappy, which is why it's important to make sure we have a broad definition of what a brand is. Using this definition we can apply these insights and those that follow to any personal, professional, organizational, or product brand.

A brand can be a . . .

- **Business:** Nike, Apple, Starbucks

- **Product:** Air Max, Apple Watch, Verisimo

- **Organization/institution:** Humane Society, Planned Parenthood, Harvard

- **Person:** Professionals, politicians, and celebrities such as Tony Robbins, Barack Obama, and Taylor Swift

- **Place:** Communities, cities, or countries such as North Carolina's Research Triangle, Chicago, the United States

- **Something undefinable:** Things that fall in the spaces

between but still need others to rally around them, like our landmarks and special causes

It's not a stretch to say that really anything in this day and age can be a brand. It doesn't matter if you're a solo entrepreneur, a corporate marketing manager for a Fortune 500 company, or a communications manager for a town of 500. We're all in the brand-building business.

Now that we have established the comforting fact that we're all brands, let's take a look at some of the misappropriations of this construct as we look for a smart solution for defining your brand.

Your brand is not just . . .

– Your logo

– Your slogan, mission statement, or whatever that nice copy under your logo says

– What your website says

– What's on your business cards

– How your employees engage customers and prospects online and off

– What others say about you

– What you do on sites like Facebook, Twitter, Pinterest, Instagram, Google+, YouTube, or the latest greatest social network

Can these items be a part of your brand? Of course. All of these items working in concert help create your brand. However, to correctly inform all of these touch points, you need a solid understanding of your brand's identity. You can't simply say that your brand is your logo or the new branding PowerPoint that your agency made for you. Many marketers grab hold of these brand fragments as it's an easy way to check that "branding thing" off the list without doing the work to ensure that, as Clow said, your brand has a belief and a soul so that you can correctly architect your messages across all forms of media.

But where do you start with this?

YOUR BRAND'S BLUEPRINT

When we were discussing the topic of branding on my podcast, Patrick Hanlon, one of the leading brand practitioners in the world and author of the books *Primal Branding* and *The Social Code*, quipped that, "Conversations about branding used to be like molding fog."[7] How can we bring this sprawling topic down to earth? We need a more systematic approach for defining our brands.

Brand building, like building anything, starts with a blueprint. Just as an architectural blueprint defines structure through design and dimensions, a brand blueprint defines who your brand is and how you tell your story. Like the girders of a skyscraper, you can't always see your brand but it's what the rest of your work stands on.

Your brand blueprint is made up of five critical elements:

- **Spark:** The spark that ignites everything your brand does, usually a single keyword such as *helping* or *innovation*. This is not a public-facing piece of your branding. Rather it's an internal keystone that anchors everything.

— **Promise:** More than a slogan, tagline, or mission statement artfully placed under your logo, a brand promise defines your ethos. Instead of being a message about you, it's a promise of what you'll do for whom.

— **Story:** From Thomas Jefferson (life, liberty, and the pursuit of happiness) to Apple (thinner, lighter, and faster), great communicators tell their stories with three key ideas.

— **Voice:** Whether it's a 140-character tweet or a 140-page e-book, words matter more than ever in marketing today. What does your brand voice sound like?

— **Visuals:** Beyond your logo, these include icons, colors, visual movement, patterns, and more.

Let's take a look at each of piece of your brand's blueprint.

The Spark That Sets Your Story in Motion

What does your brand stand for?

Branding can fall prey to checklists. You can get so consumed checking all of the identity items off your list (Business cards? *Check.* Letterhead? *Check.*) that you can forget to answer this simple question. And yet making a clear statement about what you stand for is the difference between a Mac and a PC, a Ben and Jerry's and a Häagen-Dazs, or a Nike and a Reebok. Knowing what you stand for infuses your brand with soul.

Your brand spark is the catalyst that starts this fire, not the fire itself. It activates and stimulates. It's the inspiration behind everything. Ben and Jerry's spark is social justice; it informs everything about their ice cream. Defining the intersection of technology and liberal arts is the spark that started Apple. Note that neither of these focuses solely on their product offerings of ice cream and technology. Instead, these sparks speak to bigger issues that bring these brands to life.

If you are an entrepreneur or the owner of your business, you probably have a good idea of why you got into the game. However, it may be hiding as you have every other aspect of your business from payroll to logistics on your mind. In any case, grab a legal pad—longhand is best for an exploration like this—and take a moment to write out your brand's creation story. Underline or capitalize keywords that could be your spark in hiding.

But what if you didn't start the business? If possible, find the founder or someone close to him or her and repeat the exercise above in an interview format. If you don't have access to these people, take a look at your organization and assemble a group of trusted team members who best embody your brand. Once gathered, work through defining why your brand is in business.

In the end, you should be left with a simple word (or two) that exemplifies your brand's purpose and passion such as *helping, innovation,* or *social justice.* Remember, it's your brand's fire. Only you know what kind of spark it requires.

A Promise Is More Than Pretty Words
Below Your Logo

As clever as we marketers are, it's ironic that our industry words suck as much as they do. Nowhere is this more evident than in the tired phrases we use to describe those words that sit under our

logos. Is it a tagline or a slogan? Or are you more of a mission statement type?

Slogans and taglines are predominantly promotional constructs.
At best they are campaign themes or something you roll out with a
new look. A mission statement gets us closer to your brand promise
as it relates to what you do and how you do it. However, each is burdened with excess baggage.

Slogans and taglines tend to focus on form over function. *How
does the proposed line sound? Is it "catchy" enough? And what does it look
like with the new logo?* And mission statements often get lost in the
tall grass of intellectualism—*We work to foster the ability to better
understand the importance of XYZ and how the people of X and Y including but not limited to Z are impacted. Furthermore . . .* You can imagine
where it goes from here.

In order to create a brand that stands for something, you need a
clearly distilled statement of purpose to rally your troops. The idea
of a brand promise works for many reasons. Rather than the care-
lessness implied with a tagline or slogan, a promise endows your
words with greater purpose. Who is this a promise between? Your
brand and those you serve. The power of the word "promise" is that it
brings the most important player to the forefront—your customers.
To build a brand, you must make a solemn promise to those you
serve. If the paying customers aren't at the end of what you're doing
at every level, then you're spinning your wheels.

Brand strategist Justin Foster, who has authored two books on
creating engaging brands—*Human Bacon: A Man's Guide to Creating
an Awesome Personal Brand* and *Oatmeal v. Bacon: How to Differen-
tiate in a Generic World*—has a simple definition of a brand promise,
"It's the leadership team's promise for how they'll treat the people
that touch their brands."[8] That's why a brand promise comes with a
formula. Your brand promise is *what you do for whom.* This takes the

bold catchiness from the tagline school of thought and reinforces it with the essence of a mission. You can wordsmith it all you want, but most can fill in the blanks of this very basic formula.

Zappos was built on founder Tony Hseih's desire to deliver happiness, as his book of the same title states. This philosophy anchors all of Zappos' brand communications with the promise that they are Powered by Service. Their brand promise is one of service, not shoes.

A well-crafted brand promise can embolden brand ambassadors both internally and externally. Remember, your brand isn't what you sell, say, or do. It's what you believe. The best way to unite your community around what your brand believes is to make them a promise. In addition to building your brand, this is also a key step in establishing trust, which is critical in strengthening relationships both online and off.

Tell Your Story in Three Parts

With a better understanding of what your brand is and what you stand for, it's time to tell your story. But before you prepare to write your organization's answer to *War and Peace*, get ready for a big constraint.

You only get three words to do this. And three words are all you need in most cases. In ancient times, Latin scholars decreed, *Omne trium perfectum*—everything that comes in threes is perfect, or, every set of three is complete—more commonly known as the rule of three.[9] You'll find this pattern throughout history from great political leaders and business pioneers alike. Thomas Jefferson's work of declaring independence was made easier by stating that we should all have the right to three things, "life, liberty, and the pursuit of happiness," rather than a rambling off a list of 37 grievances.

Steve Jobs famously (and obsessively) found sets of threes compelling. Most new Macs, iPhones, and iPads are still released with three different levels and often with three core benefits such as "thinner, lighter, and faster." Add to this the fact that we're now exposed to thousands of marketing messages each day and it's easy to see that we could all enhance our communication by simplifying.

When it comes to your brand, what three things can you use to tell your story? Here are—you guessed it—three different options.

- **Story Arc:** All stories have a beginning, middle, and end. Does your audience's interaction with you follow an arc that you can zero in on? For example, a consulting firm might use the stages of a typical client engagement—*identify, implement, integrate.*

- **Benefits:** We aren't here to talk about features, right? Instead, we focus on *benefits.* What are three ways that you make your customers' lives better? A breakfast bar might be *convenient, low-fat,* and *energy-packed.*

- **Philosophy:** In a more complex, service-based business or a nonprofit, your story and benefits might not be as concrete. In this situation, focus on three core philosophies that guide your organization. For example, a local homeless shelter might provide *help, healing,* and *hope.*

You'll notice that alliteration was used in a couple of the examples. If an alliterative word choice is just as descriptive as your other options, use it to tie your three words together. This is recommended for one simple reason: it's easy to remember for both your customers and your employees. Rhyming helps for the same reason. As best-selling author Daniel Pink writes in *To Sell Is Human,* "Pitches that rhyme are more sublime."[10] All of this helps increase processing fluency, or how easily our audience can understand what we've just told them.

As we'll discuss in the chapters ahead, new marketing channels such as Facebook and Twitter provide opportunities for people at all levels of your organization to be brand ambassadors. It's our job as marketers to arm them with easy-to-recall tools they can use to represent the brand. They need to be familiar with your story but they also need to know how your brand's voice sounds.

Finding Your Brand Voice

By now you may have noted that the spark isn't public-facing, the promise is a simple phrase, and the story is a boiled-down list of three words. Now what? These three elements provide a framework or foundation you can use to build your brand. From here, your brand is built primarily through the voice and visuals you use.

Brand voice is no longer the sole domain of your advertising copywriter. Everyone who is customer-facing (either online or off) should understand not only the tone of your brand's voice (casual, positive, assertive, technical) but also the vocabulary and keywords that are the building blocks of your brand's lexicon.

These keywords can serve a marketing purpose in planning and optimizing your content but they are also your brand's "sacred words," as described by Patrick Hanlon in his book *Primal Branding*.[11] When we go to Starbucks we don't order a small, medium, or large. We order a *tall, grande,* or *venti.* They've established a brand voice so strong, with such a unique vocabulary, that we've adopted it as part of our own vernacular.

While speaking at an entrepreneur expo, I met the owner and founder of the Holden Family Farm. Hailing from the small town of Scranton, Iowa, the Holden Family raises hormone-free beef. Instead of leading with this descriptive yet bland copy, they talk about their commitment to their cattle by saying that they're involved from "Conception to Consumption." Say what you will but that's a business card you don't forget. It's okay to laugh at this. The Holden Family does it with a big smile when they tell you about their brand.

Beyond specific words, your brand voice also directs how conversations are framed. If yours is a people-focused brand, you might remind those speaking on behalf of your brand that they should humanize things whenever possible and talk about "our team" or "our people" or "the people we serve." Some brands are more formal in voice while others, such as Chipotle and Old Spice, embrace humor and wit.

Think back on the last time you told your brand's story. What words stood out? How was the conversation framed? Start a list to formalize these words and distribute it internally. If your team understands why these words are important, they'll be more likely to integrate them into their own voice as well.

Choose Visuals That Tell Your Story

You'll notice that the visuals have been deliberately left to the end of our scrappy brand blueprint. That's not to say that visuals aren't important. Rather, this sequencing is essential because it's important to define who you are and what your core beliefs are before you start assigning visuals.

Your visuals start with a strong foundation—a solid logo and corporate identity. However, more than making sure that your letterhead and business cards match, in this new digital world you need to ensure that you have typography that can transcend platforms and a lexicon of app-friendly iconography as well. You also need to consider how your brand can flourish in a controlled ecosystem like your website as well as on off-site platforms such as Facebook, Twitter, Instagram, and more.

Like your brand voice, your visuals may be prescriptive and thematic. If your brand is product-focused, you'll want to build a library of high-resolution art for sharing across various channels. If your business is technical, your library will likely be composed of process graphics. If you're in the service industry or you're a nonprofit, you might want to reinforce human aspects and emotional triggers with images of people.

The point here is to have a visual bedrock in place to avoid situations where you need a Facebook cover photo or an intro slide for a YouTube video and someone just grabs a random picture. These online spaces are all opportunities that help reinforce your brand.

Your brand visuals checklist should include:

- **Branding:** Your logo plus general identity style guidelines.

- **Color considerations:** Many online platforms allow you to customize your design and colors; be prescriptive with what's on-brand and what's not.

- **Photo recommendations:** If you have original photos that should be used or preferred stock resources, point to them.

- **Technical considerations:** If your brand can be nothing more than a small, square avatar, what should it be? If you layer cover photos and avatars, as Facebook and Twitter allow, what should that combination look like?

- **Narrative considerations:** How is your brand's story depicted throughout your communications? Work on developing unique visuals that help you relay your brand's sacred words.

An off-brand visual may seem trivial. But remember, your brand is a gestalt created in your customer's mind through all of your touch points working together in concert. You can't afford to miss a single branding opportunity in today's complex digital marketplace.

UNSHARED BLUEPRINTS WON'T GET THE JOB DONE

With a blueprint in place, what happens next? If you follow the metaphor through to its logical conclusion, it's time to start building. Unshared schematics won't get the job done. This scrappy brand blueprint is purposefully simple. In addition to being easy for you to sketch out, it should be something that's easy for you to share with the rest of your team. You'll find that these two themes persist throughout this book. Scrappy marketing and the plans we make in support of it should be easy for you to both create and share. The latter—sharing with the rest of your team—is essential if you want to do more with less.

Unless you're an award-winning animation studio, you might think that there's little that you have in common with Pixar. But in the scrappy spirit of seeing ideas everywhere, consider how Pixar fosters creativity and consistency in their brand and the products they create. As outlined by co-founder Ed Catmull in his book *Creativity, Inc.*, Pixar has a "brain trust" of directors, producers, and writers who serve as an advisory council, offering candor, criticism, and essentially insight on what's on-brand for the studio and its films.[12] Could you implement a brand brain trust? McDonald's has.

Steve Levigne, vice president of U.S. strategy and insights at McDonalds USA, told me about their own brain trust. "We have a partnership between the marketing and strategy departments and our agency partners." This cross-functional team oversees all aspects of the brand with each group taking ownership and running point on different areas as needed. "We have a saying—freedom within a framework. We have frameworks that we can apply to a variety of situations."[13] You can't build your brand alone. You need flexible frameworks that you can share with your own brain trust to help you get the job done. The blueprint you develop plays that role.

To employ today's digital marketing tools, you need to think before going out of the gate. To build better brands online you need to first know who you are. As our marketing megaphone continues to change at an unprecedented rate, you need to make sure you have something solid behind it. You need to know *who* you are in order to determine *how* your story is told.

Who is only the first in a series of questions you need to answer before you dive in. The other questions—*why* and *what*—are addressed in the next two chapters as we map a path to marketing success guided by our digital compass.

 **NEXT STEPS**

Create your brand blueprint now. Use the following questions to get you started.

- Think about your brand spark. Who are you and what does your brand stand for?

- What's your brand promise? What do you do for whom?

- What three words are most important for your brand's story?

- How would you describe your brand voice?

— Apart from your logo, what other visuals are an important part of your brand? How can you better incorporate them both online and off?

— How can you share this blueprint with the rest of your team? Who should be a part of your brand's brain trust?

Chapter 2

MAP YOUR MARKETING

"Would you tell me, please, which way I ought to go
from here?" said Alice.
"That depends a good deal on where you want to
get to," said the (Cheshire) Cat.
"I don't much care where —" said Alice.
"Then it doesn't matter which way you go," said the Cat.

—Lewis Carroll, *Alice in Wonderland*[1]

The above exchange that Alice has with the Cheshire Cat as she begins her journey through Wonderland is one scrappy marketers should take under advisement. Like branding, few marketers today make real time for strategy. It's the plate of vegetables we don't want to eat. But just like those Brussels sprouts that your mom could never close the deal on, a solid strategy provides nutrients your marketing needs down the road.

Without strategy, the final leg of our journey—measuring success—will be a guess at best because we never bothered to define where it was we wanted to go. Management consultant Peter Drucker said, "You can't manage what you don't measure." The last thing I'd do is argue with Drucker, but ultimately you can't *measure* what you don't first take control of *managing*. Before we can measure, we have to manage what we're doing and why we're doing it.

In large corporate settings strategy is developed in a series of top-heavy, navel-gazing meetings after which huge swaths of the workforce are tied up in lengthy, unproductive meetings. This cumbersome process all too often results in heavy, tabbed binders containing the working plan—the Sacred Corporate Strategy—being distributed to all parties. Far from being an actionable document, the end result is usually something that sits on the shelf next to the crisis plan.

It was groupthink like this led Southwest Airlines co-founder, chairman emeritus, and former CEO Herb Kelleher to famously quip, "We have a strategic plan. It's called 'doing things.'" As clever as Kelleher's sentiment is, for most organizations, reality resides somewhere in between. Without a plan, our marketing is rudderless and impossible to evaluate. Too much planning, on the other hand, often obfuscates what really matters.

How do you overcome these organizational obstacles and create a smart strategy?

A MAP TO GET WHERE YOU'RE GOING

Like branding and eating vegetables, marketing strategy can seem like a chore. It's abstract, sprawling, and not always a whole lot of fun. But just as Alice eventually realizes, we have to get somewhere. We have a business to run, a product we need to launch, a community we need to connect with, or some other outcome we hope to influence through marketing. It can be helpful to think of marketing as a journey. At this stage, we're planning for the trip ahead. With a clearly defined brand, we need to chart our course.

A good marketing strategy is a lot like a map. That's because it gets you where you want to go and helps you find your way if you're lost. As noted in the previous chapter, the words we choose matter. In addition to the words we use publicly, internal words can have impact as well. When you say you're working on your *strategy*, coworkers might avoid you like the plague for fear of getting pulled into a never-ending series of meetings and emails. Say instead that you're *mapping out a new direction for marketing* and it not only excites your team but it makes you sit a little taller as well.

Thinking of your strategy as a map also keeps you focused on getting where you want to go rather than appealing to internal or academic ideas of what a strategy is or isn't. You need a map for pointing your marketing in the right direction, selecting the proper path, and ultimately knowing if you've arrived at your destination. No tabbed binders required.

What does a good, concise marketing map include? The answer lies in the jungle in the early 1900s.

- -
RUDYARD KIPLING, MARKETING GENIUS

As smart marketers creating a map to get where we're going, we need a formula for including the most important details. Though the basic construct was first explored by English diplomat and judge Thomas Watson and U.S. professor and preacher William Cleaver Wilkinson, it was author Rudyard Kipling who memorialized what we now call the Five Ws and One H in his poem "The Elephant's Child" from 1902's *Just So Stories*.[2]

> I keep six honest serving-men
> (They taught me all I knew);
> Their names are What and Why and When
> And How and Where and Who.

The Five Ws—who, what, when, where, and why, along with how (an honorary 'W'), or simply the "Kipling Method"—have long been practiced as critical guiding principles in journalism, research, and police investigations. This fact-based formula also holds the key to mapping your marketing success. Though it's based on ideas dating back centuries, this tried-and-true framework can help you identify the most important factors in planning your marketing.

Too often organizations launch campaigns without first consulting the six serving-men. Let's take a look at how Kipling's treasured colleagues can help you shape your brand's marketing strategy.

Why— While this is easily the most important "serving-man" in your strategy, it is often overlooked. Before setting off, take a moment and clearly and concisely define why you are doing this in the first place. Start by answering the simple question of what business goal or goals you're looking to have an impact on. *Improving customer service? Increasing brand awareness? Gaining better market insight?* It could be any number of objectives—just make sure they're clearly defined. We'll take a closer look at *why* later in this chapter.

What— With your objective in place, state *what* it is you will do. In a marketing plan, this usually spells out which channels or media you'll use to accomplish your *why*. For example, maybe you'll use Twitter for customer support or employ Snapchat for a new product launch. Though we're concentrating on emerging digital channels, it's important we consider every possible solution. This saves us from falling prey to the law of the hammer. As psychologist Abraham Maslow cautioned, "If all you have is a hammer, everything looks like a nail." As a marketer, it's easy for every tactic to look digital but that may not always be the case. Remember the example earlier about the Sewer Science newsletter that trumped something sexy and digital with highly relevant and engaging content. We'll look at how to answer this very big question in the next chapter.

Who— While this could seem like a simple answer, it actually has many layers. *Who are you? Who is responsible for carrying out your marketing campaigns? Who is responsible for execution and analysis? Who should be consulted? Who has additional oversight?* The first layer (*Who are you?*) was outlined earlier when we discussed building the brand behind the megaphone. The next layer is big. *Who are you involving in your digital marketing? Who are you serving?* Scrappy staffing is the focus of Chapter 5, while creating marketing aligned around your stakeholders' needs is discussed later in this chapter and the following chapter.

Where— An extension of *who*, this encompasses *where* your team sits in your organization. *Is your team comprised of one department or is it made up of a cross-functional group? Is this going to be addressed internally or externally via an agency? Or perhaps some hybrid of the two?* Keep in mind that *where* can also include the physical space in which your team is organized. *Are you a virtual team or will you require a brick-and-mortar setup such as a digital command center?*

When— As you dig a little deeper tactically, you'll start to answer the *when. When are your social media channels updated? Real-time? Hourly? Daily? What does your staffing and engagement schedule look like? When are you creating content?* Don't forget to nail down when you're going to review your key performance indicators or KPI (Tip: You probably won't want to review these more frequently than monthly if you want to observe real trends).

Data from Edison Research shows us that despite the fact that more than half of us check Facebook first thing in the morning and throughout the day at work, 84 percent are still active during prime-time hours with 63 percent checking right before they go to sleep. The data goes on to note that 57 percent expect the same response time regardless of the time of day.[3] The point? New channels have significant impact on the *who*, *when*, and *where* of your marketing. Don't underestimate these considerations when mapping your strategy. *Who, where* and *when* will be explored in Chapter 5 as well.

How— With a plan in place, ask yourself *how* your team is going to accomplish all of this. *What tools will they need? Are there additional resources you'll have to bring in?* And don't forget the all-important issue, *how will you measure success?* Make sure your key performance indicators are aligned with your first serving-man, *why*—your business goal for embarking on this journey in the first place. Remember, without that business objective clearly defined, your marketing will be unmeasurable. *How* is a daunting and comprehensive question to answer. That's why much of this book focuses on how we get this done.

Answering these six basic questions can give your marketing strategy a solid foundation. Can you flesh it out further? Of course, but Kipling's passage offers an easy framework to get you started as you rethink your marketing. Remember, they're called the six *serving*-men. That's because having each one in place will serve you and your organization well.

- - - - - - - - - - - - - - - - - - - -
DROPPING THE PIN IN YOUR DESTINATION

If your overall marketing strategy is your map, then your business objective is the destination you're driving toward. Without a destination, you're left going in circles. To steer your marketing in the right direction (have I overextended the metaphor yet?), you need to define the all-important *why* of the Kipling Method. *Why are we doing this? What's the business objective behind this?* As Simon Sinek explains in his TED talk and book of the same name, you have to *Start with Why*.

Having a defined business objective sets off all of the other elements in our strategy. It informs *what* we should do, *who* should be involved, *where* they are, *when* this happens, *how* all of this is executed, and *how* it is measured. Again, without a defined destination, you'll never know if you've arrived at where you need to be.

Let's say, for example, that you own a local hardware store that is getting creamed by the home improvement big box superstores, Lowe's and Home Depot. A defining feature of your brand is your knowledgeable team that has hands-on experience with what you're selling and can offer customers sound advice. Your ultimate business objective is to drive more in-store traffic over time as a result of your staff's seasoned and superior expertise.

Off the bat, this should tell you that you need to aggressively get into the local consideration set for home improvement via paid search and social advertising. Broadcast media is a costly, tough playing field to compete on when your competitor has an arsenal of TV ads featuring Ed Harris's helpful baritone driving their dominant brand awareness. Instead you'll create colloquial, engaging videos featuring local staff answering common customer questions. You'll then share these videos via social media channels, where they can be easily found by local consumers.

This strategy already identifies who's going to be involved (staff), where it happens (in-store to showcase the experience), and when (probably after hours). Most importantly, it tells you how you're going to measure success: by correlating in-store traffic with views of your online videos. You could also implement a "How did you hear about us?" initiative at checkout or use one of the other tactics we'll review in Chapter 8 when we look at measurement.

While this is a hypothetical scenario, you get the idea. With your brand blueprint packed, you need to drop a pin in your strategic map representing the destination or business objective that you're working toward.

SMART GOALS AND CAUTIONARY TALES

Remember, many simply skip strategy. These are the marketers you've spoken with who have engaged in Checklist Marketing, are experimenting with every social channel, and report that they aren't necessarily "seeing anything" when it comes to real results.

An interesting illustration offering both a best practice and a cautionary tale is the United States space program. Emboldened by President John F. Kennedy's historic speech, "I believe that this nation should commit itself to achieving the goal, before this decade is out, of landing a man on the Moon and returning him safely to the Earth," NASA set out to do just that through the Apollo program.[4] We all know what happened next.

As Chip and Dan Heath outline in *Made to Stick*, JFK created the quintessential sticky idea.[5] This single sentence is also a near-perfect example of a strategic map anchored by a solid objective. Based on those words, you have a pretty clear idea of what the boss wants, right?

- **Why (the objective):** Space exploration.

- **What:** Sending a man to the moon and returning him safely to the earth.

- **Who:** This nation.

- **Where:** Earth to the Moon.

- **When:** Before the decade is out.

- **How:** Okay, this is why I said *near*-perfect. JFK left this part of the plan for the aerospace engineers to fill in. But as for *how* this would be measured, that's pretty clear.

Before you decide to pattern your organization's strategy after the space program, consider where it is 50 years later. Like our cautionary tales of organizations lacking strategy, NASA has retired the shuttle fleet and suspended any new missions until they can get their strategic ducks in a row on where to go next. Mars? Landing on an asteroid?

But we can use President Kennedy's words as a guide for anchoring our marketing with a solid objective. By solid we mean an objective that is SMART. The SMART method, first established by George T. Doran in *Management Review,* provides a framework for defining your destination that is still useful today.[6] A SMART destination or business objective is:

- **Specific:** Focuses on something specific you want to improve

- **Measurable:** Something you can quantify or qualify to measure success

- **Attainable:** Something that can actually be done

- **Relevant:** A connection with this activity and the major goals of your organization

- **Time-related:** Bound by a specific timeline

Again, the Kennedy quote meets all criteria perfectly, but it can also be applied to businesses of all shapes and sizes. For example, a local restaurant and bar with a vibrant nightlife might want more lunch business. This can easily become a SMART objective by adding a few details such as how much you are hoping to improve sales by and what kind of time frame you're working within:

Example: *Our goal is to increase lunch business by 15 percent over the next three months.*

- *Specific:* Lunch business.

- *Measurable:* Monthly lunch receipts compared with the previous months.

- *Attainable:* 15 percent is a realistic goal given the timeline.

- *Relevant:* More lunch business means more overall food and beverage sales.

- *Time-related:* Three-month window.

A good objective shouldn't take more than a sentence. Period. These constraints are more than arbitrary. They're necessary if you want a goal that's easy for all stakeholders to understand, internalize, and help you achieve. With this objective in place, it gives you a smarter approach for looking at the other components of your marketing map.

- **Why (the objective):** *Our goal is to increase lunch business by 15 percent over the next three months.*

- **What:** Utilize Instagram and Periscope to create engaging prelunch vignettes to increase lunchtime traffic.

- **Who:** There are two key parties involved. First, our target audience—local businesses with larger workforces in need of lunch options. Second, our "stars"—our staff will be implementing this strategy.

- **Where:** In our restaurant (offline); Instagram, Periscope, Facebook, Twitter (online).

- **When:** Prior to lunch during weekdays.

- **How:** Have a local improv troupe do workshops with our waitstaff to help them produce short and specific videos featuring daily specials and containing fun, topical content about the area.

In defining a SMART destination for your marketing, let's take a look at some of the more common objectives that marketers use today.

––––––––––––––
THE SIX MOST COMMON
BUSINESS OBJECTIVES FOR MARKETERS

After striving to be hyperspecific and focused, it may seem odd to take a step back and look at generalities. However, as you work to craft your SMART marketing objective, reviewing some of the more common objectives can be a helpful place to start. If you think about it, most of what we do in marketing falls into one of six larger categories of objective: branding, public relations, community-building, market research, customer service, and leads/sales.

You may be looking at this list and thinking, "We do all of that!" That may be, but in focusing your digital marketing, start small. Select an objective or two and build your map out from there (many marketers employ a primary/secondary objective approach). To help you decide, let's take a closer look at each one.

Branding

As we discussed in Chapter 1, branding can be hard to get your arms around. As an objective it can encompass basic brand building, growing your brand, and protecting your brand. Your objective depends on what stage your brand is at. Are you a new brand entering the market or an established brand entering a new market? In either case, your branding objective will be focused on awareness-building and communicating the core messages established in your brand blueprint.

Oakland-based start-up GoldieBlox, a toy company out to inspire the next generation of female engineers, has built their business and their brand almost entirely online. "Online branding has been a key part of the growth and success of our business," said GoldieBlox founder Debbie Sterling.[7] The company launched via Kickstarter and reached their goal of raising $150,000 in just four days. This brand awareness eventually led to a call from the head buyer of construction toys at Toys R Us.[8]

"We launched on Kickstarter, continued to raise awareness of our brand through engagement with fans and customers via our social channels, and even won our very own advertisement during the Super Bowl through an online competition with Intuit. We're still a young company, and social branding and marketing has allowed us to spread our mission to a larger audience than we could have ever dreamed of."[9]

In 2002, Procter & Gamble discontinued their Vidal Sassoon line of low-cost salon-quality hair care products. As need in the marketplace emerged once again, they reintroduced the brand a decade later. Given how crowded the health and beauty category is and how complex the media landscape had gotten since the last time they had product on the shelves, Vidal Sassoon kicked off with a campaign designed to help rebuild their brand of everyday hair care. They accomplished this by inviting fans on Facebook, Twitter, and Instagram to post photos using the hashtag #ShowYourGenius. Fans who participated were rewarded with prizes, even at the most basic level, while Vidal Sassoon enjoyed a digital brand comeback.

Whether you're building from scratch or rebuilding, branding will always be a solid marketing objective.

Public Relations

Another consistent objective for marketers involves the art of public relations. With experience in reaching out to influencers and media outlets as well as in dealing with the public at large, many public relations pros have been quick to harness the power of today's digital marketing tools to scale these efforts.

The Nationwide Children's Hospital Columbus Marathon has used social media channels such as Twitter, Facebook, Instagram, and Pinterest to help engage and interact with every audience critical to the event's success, including outreach to sponsors and potential sponsors as well as participants and observers of the event itself.

"Social media helps the marathon accomplish multiple goals, including building year-round community, improving customer service, eliminating the 'scare' factor for first-time marathoners, and supporting registration goals," said Heather Whaling, whose firm Geben Communication works alongside the marathon's PR agency to manage the social media aspects of the event. "Since The Columbus Marathon decided to take a proactive, strategic approach to social media, the event has sold out faster and faster each year, while continuing to expand the field of participants. At the same time, social media allows the event to provide an additional channel to connect sponsors with participants."[10]

Social media can also serve as a great quick-response mechanism when you find yourself in a public-relations firestorm. When one of their planes landed nose first at LaGuardia in 2013, Southwest Airlines began issuing statements immediately via Facebook and Twitter to control the story and the flow of news. While it's easy to look at situations and say, "Yep, we'll use social media if that happens," the only way to ensure success is to have a plan already in place.

With tools like Facebook and Twitter, the lines between marketing and PR are more blurred than ever for many organizations. However, digital media offers us an array of powerful new tools we can use to get the right story and narrative in front of our customers and community.

Community Building

Among the new opportunities digital marketing has brought about is the ability to cultivate and grow online communities. We don't simply talk at our fans and customers anymore. We have conversations with them that help us build community. Ultimately, as evidenced in the story of GoldieBlox, a passionate, brand-driven community can be a powerful way to connect people and create an army of brand ambassadors. But how does one go about accomplishing this objective?

New Belgium Brewing is a great example of a scrappy brand for many reasons. First, in addition to their main Instagram and Twitter accounts, the Fort Collins, Colorado-based brewery has nearly 30 local Instagram and Twitter pages across more than a dozen strategic local markets. This doesn't sound as daunting when you consider the fact that these pages are maintained by their local field marketers—brand ambassadors—in each state. Those same field marketers also post geo-targeted messages from the main New Belgium Facebook page.

"The content on the local pages is controlled by the field marketer living in that market," says Kevin Darst of New Belgium. "They know the region/city better than we do, so it is better that they contribute the regular content. We do have a content calendar for things that are nationally relevant: new beer releases, national events, significant New Belgium Brewing cultural happenings, etc. But for the most part the field marketers are handed the keys and told to own their market."[11]

Your community isn't always homogeneous, either. Another option when it comes to community building is creating custom content around subgroups within your community. Sporting goods retailer Scheels does a great job of this through their Scheels Community Blog, which houses content across a wide variety of affinity and interest areas complementing the chain's major offerings, from bass-fishing and archery to camping and fitness. In addition to helpful content written by expert contributors, each area also features a "brag board" where fans can post their latest catch or outdoor accomplishment.

This connected hive of followers can be a tremendous asset. That's why community building has emerged as a critical marketing objective for brands of all shapes and sizes.

Market Research

Another advantage of the multidirectional conversations we now enjoy with our community is the fact that we can use them to help improve our products and services. Traditionally, marketers had to rely on formal research and focus groups to gather consumer insights. Today we can launch surveys using tools like Survey Monkey to gather feedback on products, services, and events using social media channels to ask questions.

Taken to the extreme, Starbucks has built a massive idea engine using Salesforce's Force.com platform. My Starbucks Idea (mystarbucksidea.com) provides fans with opportunities to share, view, and vote on ideas for how to improve the Starbucks experience. These ideas range from menu suggestions ("Have the pumpkin spice latte available all year round") to promotional improvements ("Free drinks should not expire so quickly"). Finally, community members can view "Ideas in Action" that have been implemented by Starbucks. Since launching in 2008, My Starbucks Idea has had over 150,000 ideas submitted from customers. This social site has delivered countless innovations and successes to the coffee giant, including the "skinny" beverage, digital rewards through the Starbucks Card, and free WiFi.[12]

Before you hang your head and fall prey to the Myth of Big, you should know that you don't have to create a crowd-sourcing idea site to build close relationships with your community. Businesses of all sizes can gain greater transparency and trust while conducting a bit of market research via their Facebook page and other social sites. Simply asking questions about what you could improve or having customers vote between your two finalists for a new package design or product name can go a long way toward building community and conducting market research.

Customer Service

In the book *The Now Revolution*, authors Jay Baer and Amber Naslund refer to social media as "the new telephone," issuing a stern warning to us all that we must remember to answer it.[13] This metaphor is applicable to the business objective of customer service and support as well. Essentially, if customer service is a need you have across other channels, you must ensure that you are answering your social support line as well.

Businesses of all shapes and sizes are using the social telephone to right wrongs online and off. New Pioneer Co-op, a natural food store and bakehouse in Iowa City, Iowa, used a bit of online customer service to intervene in an offline issue. Recently, while on a quick lunch date, my wife experienced a problem with her deli sandwich that wasn't corrected by the staff on site. I did what any digitally savvy husband would do and took to Twitter to complain about the experience. Within minutes, the co-op engaged with a bit of good humor (I may have called the deli workers "sammich hippies" in the heat of the moment), took the matter offline, and had a gift card out by the end of the week. This story isn't particularly remarkable. It was classic customer service in action. What's noteworthy is that this journey began offline in the store, was addressed online through social media, and was ultimately made right through an old-fashioned gift card delivered via snail mail.

Warby Parker is changing the way we purchase glasses by shifting as much of the experience online as possible. Customers are sent frames at home to try on before purchasing. As this is a complex purchase that usually involves a lot of questions in-store, Warby Parker steps up to the plate online with answers as well. When someone tweets a question about a particular frame they receive a reply with a custom video from the team addressing them by name, showing them the glasses up close, answering questions, and making recommendations based on their selection. A point worth driving home is the fact that these are *custom* videos, not simply canned responses about their frames. The short videos usually begin with a rep calling you by name and answering *your* questions. What an effective way of delivering highly personalized service.

Even if customer service isn't a core component of your business model, you should be prepared for the fact that your community will talk back and can now find you if they need you. Will you be ready for them?

Leads and Sales

Cha-ching! Making money from the Internet! Woo-hoo! This is usually where most marketers perk up with excitement in their eyes. If you skipped the other objectives and came straight here, you should go back and at least learn about the others as there are both indirect and direct ways of influencing your bottom line online, which we'll examine further when we discuss measurement in Chapter 8.

That said, generating leads and sales is a legitimate need for many. The marketers at Scratch Cupcakery, a four-location cupcake bakery in Iowa, focus on driving in-store traffic with their social media activity through updates containing new product information, in-store events, and special offers and sales. "We have been very intentional about only offering deals via social media—never in print," explains owner Natalie Brown. "Our offers don't require printing or scanning of a bar code—they are measured in foot traffic. Word spreads quickly—we've seen upwards of 450,000 views on a single deal post. We have gone from a relatively busy day to complete insanity in a number of minutes after posting a great deal. Our social offers double our in-store traffic and cause spikes in future orders as well."[14]

Businesses in the more complex world of B2B may find themselves focusing on lead generation rather than direct sales. Kinvey, a "Backend as a Service" platform that makes it easy for developers to set up, use, and operate a cloud backend for their mobile apps, uses engaging content to drive leads. Their e-book "How to Make an App: Android Edition" is responsible for 40 percent of the new accounts that are opened.[15]

Lead generation and sales can also be a business objective in a complex industry such as the automotive sector. Ford has been a social media pioneer since their Fiesta Movement, featuring driver-generated content. They also accomplished another industry first by launching their redesigned Explorer on Facebook rather than competing with the rest of the marketplace noise at a traditional auto show. The result allowed them to dominate the news for a day and, more importantly, generate buzz and capture new leads for their dealers.

Regardless of which stage of the sales funnel you focus on, lead generation and sales drives business for many.

DON'T MAKE THIS MISTAKE

It's important to remember your customers' needs in mapping your strategy and determining your objective as well. Sounds pretty obvious, right? And yet, once again, many marketers miss the forest for all the trees.

As first identified by Brian Solis and Pivot, the perception gap is "very real and very deep." While 76 percent of marketers feel they know what their customers want, only 34 percent have bothered to ask.[16] The data goes on to show that there are major areas of disconnect, including the fact that customers actually want more special offers, coupons, and deals online than marketers think they do.

Rather than being reactive with your audience and retrofitting your objective to their needs, start from scratch and look at those needs from the beginning. Establish customer profiles or personas for each of your key audience segments that include both quantitative and qualitative insights. Use this as a touchstone as you work through your overall marketing strategy.

Remember, your brand promise defines what you do for whom. Building that solid foundation should ensure that your marketing is grounded in audience need and SMART business objectives. With a clear destination in mind, let's take a look at how to get smart with *what* marketing tools you choose to help you get where you're going.

 NEXT STEPS

It's time to create your scrappy marketing map. What destination are you driving toward?

- Which objective makes the most sense for you—branding, public relations, community building, market research, customer service, or lead generation/sales?

- Does your map's marketing objective pass the SMART test? Is it:

  - *Specific*

  - *Measurable*

- *Attainable*

- *Relevant*

- *Time-related*

- Don't forget to ask your customers what kind of communications would be most beneficial to them. In fact, send an email or ask them via social media right now. It's that simple.

Chapter 3

FOLLOW YOUR DIGITAL COMPASS

In the 1997 movie *The Edge*, penned by Pulitzer Prize-winning playwright David Mamet, the main characters Charles and Bob (played respectively by a cerebral Sir Anthony Hopkins and cynical Alec Baldwin) find themselves lost in the Alaskan wilderness. Their survival is further complicated by a man-killing bear (deftly played by Bart the Bear—whose illustrious career you should look up). As tensions run high, Baldwin's Bob starts to lose it while Hopkins's Charles coolly asserts that they can walk out of the woods on their own.

Charles tells Bob that most people who die in the wilds die of shame that they got themselves into such a situation. "And so they sit there and they die," he says. "Because they didn't do the one thing that would save their lives." When asked what that one thing is, Charles replies, "Thinking."[1]

Thinking. Putting our brains before our budget. Looking before we leap. These are the smart steps that have led us to this point. In looking back, the allusions to marketing as a journey have been plentiful. Before you could start, you had to know who you are—

– – –

what your brand is and what it stands for. With that blueprint safely packed, you mapped your marketing, dropping a pin in your desired destination—the business objective that matters most. But how do you get there?

This scene from *The Edge* also sets us up what we need to do next as marketers. After reminding Bob that they need to think, Charles walks the talk by creating a makeshift compass using a paperclip as a needle, which he magnetizes with his wool clothing before placing it in a leaf filled with water, starting them on their path out of the woods toward their desired destination.

You may not be lost in the wild, stalked by a killer bear, but you too have to get out of the woods—the wilderness of your confusion. You need to create a digital marketing compass to save you from all of the distracting Shiny New Things on the path ahead. As new social networks emerge, such as Snapchat and Periscope, it's easy to find yourself wandering off course. These side trips may be interesting, they may feel like you're going somewhere, but they may in fact be taking you in the wrong direction.

How can you create a digital marketing compass to help you stay on the right path?

YOUR DIGITAL MARKETING COMPASS

In the last chapter, we used Kipling's "six serving-men" to get started. By mapping your marketing with *why, what, who, when, where,* and *how,* you can ground your strategy. The first step was answering the *why,* dropping a pin in your destination, which represents the business objective you want to achieve. Next you need to approach *what* you're going to do to get there. *Is this best accomplished with a Facebook page? Does a blog make sense? How do we know if something like Snapchat is worth our time?*

Today, the maps that most of us use are on our smartphones. Once you've decided on your destination, the app calculates your route. If you take a wrong turn, it simply recalculates. Before GPS put navigation in the palm of your hand, you would use a compass to point you in the right direction. You need to dust off that concept and put it to work for your marketing.

Take a moment and think about a compass. The design is pretty simple. The four cardinal directions—north, south, east, west—and a magnetized needle. The earth's magnetic fields guide the needle to true north, enabling navigation. For your marketing compass, I want you to think of your marketing objective as the true north. It's where you want your needle to point. That needle represents Kipling's *what*. What are you doing to accomplish that business objective—the *why*? The magnetic fields steering your *what* in the right direction toward the true north of your objective are the rest of the serving-men—*who*, *where*, *when*, and, ultimately, *how*.

Who are we trying to reach? Where are they? When are they available? How can we get in front of them with the tools that we have? Answering these questions enables you to more accurately navigate your way through and around the Shiny New Things you encounter on the path ahead. To keep your marketing on the right path you need to focus on *what* helps you achieve your *why*.

Anything else risks taking you off course.

How to Use Your Compass

At the time of this writing, podcasting is experiencing a renaissance. Some would call it a comeback, but if you look at Edison Research's Share of Ear data you'll see that listenership has been on a steady climb over the past decade.[2] However, with the success of *Serial* in 2014, one of the first mainstream podcasting hits, marketers began diving in and creating their own podcasts. In some cases, this made sense. Others led to lost marketers chasing after Shiny New Things.

Not so with HubSpot. The inbound marketing and sales software company launched a new podcast in the wake of *Serial*, but did so for very specific reasons. HubSpot is a leading product for marketers, helping them plan and execute social media marketing, email marketing, content, web analytics, and search engine optimization among other things. As such, they have a dedicated following among marketers. Through their various blogs, they serve several core audiences, such as marketing and sales professionals, as well as advertising and marketing agencies. (Articles include "Which SEO Tactics You Should Try Next" and "4 Tips to Master the Art of Upselling and Cross-Selling.") With helpful content designed around their various audiences' needs, they are attracting a wider—and loyal—audience; this alone is a win for the digital compass.

Which brings us back to podcasting. Rather than representing a Shiny New Thing they had to try out, HubSpot had a very different need. In driving toward their objective of software adoption, they discovered something. "We realized we had an additional audience—a buyer persona—that we weren't talking to with our blog," said HubSpot podcast producer Dave Gerhardt. This audience was C-level leadership. This segment not only cared about in-the-trenches inbound marketing; they also cared about more broad-based business topics such as leadership and sales. "This audience is less likely to sit in front of the computer and read our blog, but a podcast is a great way to reach them while they're on the go," Gerhardt continued. "Based on all of this we decided that this segment would be best served by a podcast, which would allow us to reach people while they're in the car on their way to work, at the gym, or even just doing stuff around the house."[3] And that's

how *The Growth Show* was born (listen at http://www.hubspot
.com/podcast).

Each week, HubSpot sits down with someone who has achieved
remarkable growth, creating an invaluable resource for leaders who
are consumed with driving growth at their businesses—the key
audience HubSpot wanted to reach. Podcasting wasn't a good fit just
because it was in every other marketing headline. It was a good fit
because HubSpot's digital compass pointed them in the right direction. They knew *why* they were doing this (brand awareness, lead
generation among top-level execs). They knew that *what* they chose
needed to be designed around *who* their audience is and *where* and
when they could find them.

Navigating marketing today isn't hard if you have the right tools.
Using this framework, you can evaluate any new channel or platform,
filtering out the Shiny New Things and focusing on what makes the
most sense for you.

- - - - - - - - - - - - - -
THE COMPASS IN ACTION:
WHAT WORKS BEST WHEN

As any smart marketer will quickly tell you, there's no one-size-
fits-all approach for selecting the right channels to use. If anything,
quite the opposite. Only you know what works best for your business
to accomplish your unique objectives. However, given our compass
framework, we can explore a few popular paths for *what* works best
when.

As you'll see from the concise case studies that follow, while all
of Kipling's serving-men are critical, knowing *why* we're doing this
(objective) and *who* we're trying to reach (audience) helps direct us
toward the appropriate *what*. Let's take a look at a few examples of
what works best *when*.

Social Media Marketing Paths

With Edison Research reporting that 73 percent of Americans age 12 and up have a profile on a social network, it's not a big leap to say that social media has had a huge impact on how we build brands and grow businesses.[4] Like all Shiny New Things, it's important to find the network that works best for you and your audience.

Facebook— With well over a billion users, Facebook is officially larger than any country in the world in terms of population. There are more people on Facebook than there are cars in the world. I bring this up not to start comparing social network statistics, but rather as a means of noting that if your audience is fairly broad and you only have the resources to engage on one social network, there's a pretty good chance it should be Facebook. Everyone is there. Even if you aren't trying to reach everyone, Facebook's paid advertising features offer increasingly sophisticated targeting tools. However, Facebook's classic features—starting conversations, sharing content—make it a powerful tool for building community as well.

Moosejaw Mountaineering is an online and brick-and-mortar retailer specializing in outdoor recreation apparel and gear for snowboarding, rock climbing, hiking, and camping. Moosejaw is also known for its nonsensical marketing, which they candidly refer to as "Moosejaw Madness." As you can imagine, this madness is prevalent on many of their social networks but is especially well represented on their Facebook page, a quick scan of which reveals as many posts about naked pancake photos and quotes from the movie *Kingpin* as it does dry product updates.

Compass points: Why is Moosejaw using Facebook? To build community (*why*) among their customers (*who*). Online stores have to work even harder to create brands that people want to hear from and engage with. While you can create fun content on any number of social networks, where do most of your friends post funny stuff?

Twitter— While Twitter boasts just over half of Facebook's user numbers, the 140-character microblogging service has something else going for it. According to Edison data, despite the fact that less than a quarter of Americans have an account on Twitter, over half of us acknowledge hearing about tweets in the news and popular culture.[5] Twitter is a real-time marketing powerhouse that punches above its weight class. That said, it's not a great fit for every business. It all comes down to knowing why you're there. What's your business objective?

Like many businesses—from airlines and cable companies to natural food co-ops—customer service is a key need for website hosting and cloud services provider Media Temple. I found this out on my own one evening when I embarked on a late-night DIY project, building a website for a side venture of mine. The problem? While I consult, speak, write, and teach about the marketing side of technology, I really can't code a website. But I thought I could buy a domain and install the WordPress content management system on it using my Media Temple grid-hosting service. I was wrong. I broke my site. As it was the middle of the night, I tweeted customer service expecting nothing. What I received—and when I received it—was surprising.

"Being a customer-first company, we are committed to providing 24/7 people-powered support to every customer across all our support channels, including on Twitter," said TJ Stein, senior director, customer support, at Media Temple. "Media Temple was the first hosting company to use Twitter to provide timely help to customers who cannot call but still require urgent assistance. We try really hard to have problems solved on the first contact with the customer, which usually works for smaller issues, but, for bigger or more sensitive issues, a deeper, offline conversation might be needed."[6] In short, because of their exceptional Twitter support, I fixed my broken site in the middle of the night, enabling this crazy person to share it with the world amidst blurred vision and yawns.

Compass points: Why is Media Temple using Twitter? To provide customer service (*why*) to their customers *who* are having issues at all hours. When it comes to customer service, it's all about speed and overdelivering. Media Temple uses Twitter to provide both. Twitter video—both in native form and via their supporting networks Vine (six-second video loops) and Periscope (live-streaming video)—also provides marketers with useful content creation utilities. For some good examples, see how *USA Today* stays topical with Vines celebrating daily occasions such as National Donut Day. Also check out General Electric, which used Periscope to live-stream updates from the Paris Aviation Show.

LinkedIn— With all of the buzz usually reserved for Facebook and Twitter, it's easy to forget that LinkedIn is the oldest social network (that was where I created my first social media profile—back when you had to prove that you weren't just using the network to find another job!). It's also one that many marketers struggle with personally and professionally. *I just don't check LinkedIn as much as I check Facebook.* That's okay. Most people don't. These networks couldn't be more different. While Facebook is where we keep in constant communication with our personal tribe of family and friends, LinkedIn serves as our Rolodex. A collection of professional connections. It's no wonder the platform is a great fit for B2B content sharing and lead generation. However, in the spirit of seeing ideas everywhere, let's take a look at a creative, objective-driven LinkedIn use that might surprise you.

I have a secret for you: one of the most innovative companies using LinkedIn is Secret. Yes, that Secret. The women's antiperspirant. But they're not using LinkedIn to sell deodorant or talk about body odor (thank goodness). Instead, they're using LinkedIn to build their brand. Specifically, they are capitalizing on issues related to feminism and women in the workplace. One look at the description on their company page makes this clear: *Secret Clinical Strength can help keep you be 100 percent fearless at work. Check out the stories, videos and other content below for more ways to stay fearless.* "Secret is pulling the engagement lever by building a legion of loyal female customers," says Jason Miller, senior manager of global content marketing at LinkedIn. "Their whole aim is to inspire women with links to powerful female-friendly content around the web."[7]

Compass points: Why is Secret using LinkedIn? To build their brand (*why*) among women in the workplace (*who*). Other LinkedIn features not to lose sight of include groups, which are great for starting conversations and convening communities around professional roles and needs. LinkedIn has also added a blogging feature that allows marketers and thought leaders to publish content directly on this high-traffic network.

Pinterest— Another social network that is very focused in terms of audience is Pinterest. At its core Pinterest is nothing new. Social bookmarking was one of the earliest forms of social media. What Pinterest added was a highly engaging visual patchwork, creating a fun means of discovery and information search. It's no secret that Pinterest is incredibly popular among women. The most popular categories on Pinterest include food and drink, DIY and crafts, women's apparel, home decor, and travel. That's why brands focusing on lifestyle and event-driven categories have found success on Pinterest. That's not to say that other industries can't use their compass to find their way to Pinterest.

For example, Constant Contact helps small businesses and non-profits succeed with email marketing. As a B2B technology company, it's the very opposite of the categories previously referenced that are winning at pinning. However, Constant Contact has thousands of followers and hundreds of likes across their 121 Pin boards. Among the brand's more popular boards is one titled "Quotes for Small Business Owners." These regular doses of inspiration are designed with their core customer demographics in mind. While aspirational content can be shared anywhere online, the big, bold images on Pinterest get attention and engage as they inspire users to solve problems and dream big.

Compass points: Why is Constant Contact using Pinterest? To build their brand and a community (*why*) of small business owners (*who*). Our scrappy mindset urges us to see ideas everywhere. Don't stereotype social networks like Pinterest and LinkedIn based on broad assumptions. Remember, website traffic driven by Pinterest is right up there with referrals from Google and Facebook. In many cases, the average order size is greater and the frequency is higher for Pinterest users when compared with these other sources.

Instagram— Despite being one of the most basic and stripped-down social apps built entirely around sharing artfully filtered photos, Instagram is currently the fastest-growing social network and has enjoyed diverse adoption from small businesses to the Interbrand 100. This same simplicity can confound marketers wondering what they could possibly do on this very basic social network. However, just as diverse as the types of businesses using Instagram are what they're actually using it for. In fact, if you try hard enough and think visually, you can accomplish each and every one of our six marketing objectives discussed in the previous chapter. You can even generate leads and sales.

A classic marketing strategy in the consumer packaged goods sector has been to drive additional product use by sharing recipes. Chobani Greek Yogurt uses their Instagram account for just that. Among their more popular images are photos sharing recipes and other snack tips. While this doesn't instantly make the cash register ding, these visuals, like those found on Pinterest, educate, inspire, and help drive sales. "I'm thankful to have a really useful product," says Chobani Social Media Strategist Ashley Butler.[8]

Compass points: Why is Chobani using Instagram? To build their brand and drive product sales (*why*) among current and prospective customers (*who*) who may not have realized they could use the product in a particular way. A picture is worth a thousand words. Can visuals help you accomplish your marketing objectives?

Snapchat— At the time of this writing, Snapchat is the ultimate Shiny New Thing (the funny thing about "shiny and new" is that nothing holds this mantle for long—I'm sure some up-and-comer will have usurped it by the time this book is in print). However, right now it's a textbook example. Snapchat stats crowd our headlines, including the fact that nearly half of the network's users are in the coveted millennial demographic. With such a meteoric rise, most brands are left with more questions than answers when it comes to using Snapchat for business.

Our compass doesn't have to work too hard to see that it's a great fit for targeting millennials as Taco Bell has done. Because the social network's ephemeral updates (playfully known as "snaps") disappear after a preset time, you can also strategically use Snapchat to launch new products as Acura did with their NSX supercar. Like the old days of the auto industry when you would literally get a sneak peek behind the curtain, Snapchat makes that special access and exclusivity possible in the digital age. Offering a sneak peek to their first 100 Snapchat followers—who may not be in the target demographic—may seem questionable, but this strategy led to an early wave of industry media coverage.[9]

Compass points: Why is Acura using Snapchat? To generate interest and excitement (*leads*) among their current customers and prospects (*who*), specifically their inner circle of early adopters on Snapchat (the teaser video was eventually posted on Twitter and YouTube).

Content Marketing Paths

The Content Marketing Institute and MarketingProfs have been studying the rapidly evolving content marketing landscape for several years. In that time they've found that approximately 90 percent of marketers across all sectors (B2B, B2C, nonprofit) employ content marketing in some form, be it a blog, podcast, video, or newsletter.[10] Despite this rapid growth, their annual study also reports a disconnect between using content and actually having a content strategy. In fact, their most recent data shows that more than half of marketers using content are flying blind without any documented strategy.

Do we need to have Anthony Hopkins yell at them? Do the one thing that can save you and your marketing. *Think.* How can you use your digital compass to guide your content marketing? While HubSpot's podcast gave us a good example of podcasting with purpose, let's look at popular paths and compass points for blogging and videos.

Blogging — After talking about all of the Shiny New Things, it could seem that blogging is decidedly less shiny. While it has existed as a medium since the 1990s, it's still packing quite a punch as a part of the marketing mix. HubSpot's own State of Inbound Marketing has consistently reported that marketers who prioritize blogging enjoy positive return on investment (ROI), higher website traffic, and ultimately generate more leads.[11] A company blog can serve as the hub of your brand's content strategy. So how do you know if blogging is right for you?

As the juicy center of your content marketing, your blog should help your customers solve their problems. As Ann Handley and C.C. Chapman state in their book *Content Rules*, "Good content should share or solve, not shill."[12] As a leading multinational human resource consulting firm, ManpowerGroup recognized that employment law was a challenging topic for their customers. That's why they started an employment blog. Or, more specifically, The Employment Blawg (see what they did there?), led by the company's Chief Legal Officer Mark Toth.

Beyond the clever play on words in the blog's name, ManpowerGroup gets extra points for having a sense of humor about a necessarily dry topic. As the site's welcome message says, "We at Manpower believe this site is truly unique. For the first time in recorded history, a lawyer is doing something for free. This blog—or blawg—is designed to provide you with up-to-the-minute employment law information without putting you to sleep. Take a look around. You'll find entertaining videos, provocative questions, practical tools, legal alerts—even an employment law sing-along. We'll do everything we can to keep you up on the law and out of jail." Talk about voice! Remember the importance of having a brand behind the megaphone? ManpowerGroup's blog goes from good to great by not only following their compass and helping their customers but doing so with some heart and soul.

Compass points: Why is Manpower using blogging? To build their brand and position their expertise (*why*). Over time, this should lead to additional leads and sales (a second *why*) among their target audience of HR and recruiting managers (*who*).

Videos— In going through this list, you could call me out for not being parallel and listing YouTube as a social network. While users generate billions of views on YouTube each day, making it the second largest search engine in the world, its use as a stand-alone social network is dubious at best due to spammy comments and distracting related content. However, video is a popular form of content that brands can share on a variety of outlets, including YouTube, Vimeo, Facebook, and Twitter. More than a channel strategy for YouTube, you need a content strategy for your videos.

Like all forms of content, customer service and support is key. Much to my wife's chagrin, when that cold Iowa winter sets in, I become a bit of a beard enthusiast. Recently, I decided I should invest in this hobby a bit more. Various online sites and forums (more useful content!) suggested using beard oil to moisturize and promote growth. After a rigorous search (read: choosing the label I thought was the coolest), I decided on Grave Before Shave beard oil from the good folks at Fisticuffs Mustache Wax (specifically the Viking scent). A few days later, thanks to Amazon Prime, I had a small bottle and dropper in my hands. Now what?

A quick trip to the Fisticuffs site led me to a section featuring how-to videos. After just a click I was watching David, a man whose beard was mighty enough to dispense advice on the subject, explain and demonstrate the proper way to oil one's beard. Too much information? Perhaps. An extreme example? Think again. If a small company selling boutique beard oil can find an on-brand strategy for video, you can too!

Compass points: Why is Fisticuffs Mustache Wax using video? To provide customer service (*why*) to budding beard aficionados like me (*who*).

Are there other forms of content? Yes. Will new social networks emerge, perhaps displacing those previously noted? Absolutely. I've tried to hit the high points, the middle of the bell curve, at the time of this writing. Beyond the social media and content marketing tools outlined here, there are other digital tools that can be useful, such as email marketing and paid search and social media advertising. We'll explore all of these further in Chapter 6. There are also traditional tools that still pack a powerful punch, such as television (budget permitting), which can converge nicely with your digital content and conversations.

Today's digital media tools change at such a rapid pace that providing an encyclopedia of each and every channel isn't as useful as providing a system for selecting which tools to include in your mix. By using your digital compass and answering the compass points of why you're doing this (*objective*) and who you're trying to reach (*audience*), you'll have a better idea of what works best when. Don't lose sight of brands like Secret and Constant Contact, which are doing great things in unexpected places. To get scrappy, you have to get smart and see ideas everywhere.

Plans vs. Planning

With a skeletal framework in place using the Kipling Method, it's time to start putting your strategic map together. Committing your plan to a formal document can be daunting. With a physical manifestation of what you're doing on the books, it can be easier for internal naysayers to nitpick—either the content of your plan or the form it takes. It can also feel very concrete and permanent. Don't worry about this. For starters, real plans that prescribe action—as your marketing map does—can be scary for others in your organization. The bold steps you've planned and are ready to take may remind others of their own insecurities and inaction. They might even poke fun at your plan's format.

It doesn't matter what your final document looks like. Remember, overly bureaucratic organizations have ruined the expectations associated with strategy. Unless it's a huge binder that goes *thunk* when you drop it on a desk, it's somehow not up to the challenge. This is simply not true. Your strategy could be contained on a napkin or a few sheets of paper casually tossed in a folder. Or the notes in the back of this book. Even if you're feeling formal, you should still work to keep your map down to a few pages. Why? Because it's easier to write at length than it is to be concise. Use this constraint to sharpen your vision and create a plan that can guide your work and be shared with your team for easy buy-in.

To be clear, those internal nitpickers will still pick. Especially with a strategic map that looks so different from the other binders that are stacked up on their office shelves next to the crisis plan. That's why in addition to doing all of this you need to educate them on why it's important to focus on maps and getting to where we want to go instead of binders, meetings, and plans that we load up like flatbed trucks. By leading the discussion on what a strategy should be, you'll also insulate yourself from attacks on what it's not.

You should also go into your mapmaking endeavors with the idea that you are creating a living, breathing document that recalculates your route to your final destination like a GPS. As Duct Tape Marketing's John Jantsch says in his book *The Commitment Engine,* "Plans aren't the secret. Planning is. It's the continuing process of planning, acting, and measuring that moves the organization in the direction of its goals, not the plan document you might create. "[13]

Internal and external environmental factors change constantly in marketing. Especially when it comes to the emerging channels in our complex digital world. You don't know that a new network won't emerge or that there won't be a new form of content that your community will find even more engaging than Facebook posts and videos (just try writing a book about all of this!). That's why the mapmaking process provides a general marketing framework as opposed to a channel-specific prescription. This framework will also help us down the road when it's time to measure what matters. You'll only know what matters if you've done your homework.

These smart steps are skipped by many marketers. You can't afford to. If you want to do more with less, you have to first have a plan in place. To echo Jantsch, your strategy isn't the document. It's the ideas you organize around accomplishing a specific business objective. In the end, a marketing strategy or map should do one thing: get you where you're trying to go. By using Kipling's questions as the guiding forces of your digital compass you've taken a first big step toward scrappier marketing. You've put your brains before your budget and developed a system to make sense of all of the Shiny New Things that could distract you. Where are we going next? With a smart plan or map in place, it's time to focus on doing the work.

How can we market like a mousetrap—effectively and efficiently—and do more with less? How can we overcome the myth that only big brands with big teams and big budgets can do big things?

 **NEXT STEPS**

Now's the time to get started making your map.

— Think about the business objective or destination that you
   established earlier. What marketing can you create in support of that?

— What digital channels make the most sense? Use your digital compass. Why are you doing this? What's your business
   objective? Who are you trying to reach? These compass
   points will help you determine what works best when.

— Don't forget to see ideas everywhere. Forget social network
   demographics and stereotypes from your industry. Could
   you use an unexpected social site or form of content to reach
   your customers and make your organization stand out in an
   unexpected way?

— **Hint:** If you have marketing initiatives that aren't aligned
   with your objective—that could take you off course—consider eliminating them. If they don't help you accomplish
   your primary or secondary objective, why are you spending
   time and other resources on them?

Part Two

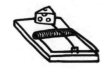

DO MORE WITH LESS

Chapter 4

CREATE A QUESTION ENGINE

When I talk with marketers at organizations small and large, I ask a lot of questions. Among the most common is a variation on "How are your current efforts performing?" As I listen to the answer, I often get an image in my head of the Apollo 11 astronauts planting the American flag on the moon. Like the space program we used as planning inspiration back in Chapter 2, we've planted our flag in this new frontier—perhaps a shiny new Facebook page or blog—but we're not sure what happens next. Or how often it should happen.

Google's Eric Schmidt turned heads when he revealed that, "Every two days we create as much information as we did from the dawn of time up until 2003."[1] Google would know too. Their biggest business unit, paid search engine advertising, is tied to how consumers search and find what they're looking for online. Google's Zero Moment of Truth research tells us that consumers are now seeking out twice as many sources of content in support of purchase decisions compared to just a few years ago.[2] Combine this data with the fact that Edison's Infinite Dial study reports that over 50 percent of Americans are checking social media constantly (several times a day) and it's no wonder that just keeping up with customers' wants and needs is chief among the concerns marketers today face.[3]

We have a plan. We know *who* we are. We've defined the brand behind the megaphone. We know *why* we're doing this. We've mapped our marketing and determined our destination. We know *what* we're doing. We've used our digital compass to tell us what channels work best when. But *how* does this work get done?

This question is fitting for a few reasons. First, it reminds us of the journey that we're on. Digital marketing tools provide us with a powerful opportunity to create conversations, content, and community that connect, engage, educate, and inform our customers. And yet we find ourselves stuck. We've planted that social media or content marketing flag, but we can't keep up with increasing consumer demands and behavior online. We're also overwhelmed by the Myth of Big. *How can we possibly keep up when only big brands with big budgets, big teams, and big tools can do big things?* This myth plagues businesses both small and large. As Alan Weiss, author of *Million Dollar Consulting*, famously quipped, "There's always a bigger boat." We can always look up and see a competitor or simply a business we admire with more resources and feel ourselves weighed down and helpless.

Instead of getting overwhelmed, we need to get scrappy! We need to create marketing that's more like a mousetrap—more effective and efficient than ever! We have to develop a system for doing more with less so we can overcome that Myth of Big. To do this, we have to break down the work of social media and content marketing first. From here, we'll use the next two chapters to look at how we can embrace our people power and connect our digital dots to help us get the most from our marketing.

To get our social media and content marketing efforts in gear, we have to create a sustainable engine capable of producing engaging content and conversations on an ongoing basis. It's also noteworthy that "How do we get the work done?" is itself a question. As we'll discuss in this chapter, building an engine powered by questions can help you create the marketing you need to arrive at your destination and accomplish your goals effectively and efficiently while informing, educating, and entertaining your customers.

However, before we talk about questions, we first need to take a step back and listen.

LISTENING FIRST

It's admittedly a tired stereotype. In TV shows and movies, we are beaten over the head with images of the therapist repeating questions back to the patient for comic effect. "What do *you* think about that?" As a fictitious talk radio therapist, Kelsey Grammer's Frasier Crane famously began each of his broadcasts with the iconic phrase, "I'm listening." We give a lot of lip service to listening to customers, but are you *really* listening?

If you cast aside all of the social media talking heads, the biggest way in which channels like Facebook and Twitter are different from traditional broadcast media is the fact that they are multidirectional in nature. Simply put, this means that rather than crafting the perfect 30-second TV spot and blasting it one-way at whoever may be watching, you are now starting conversations and creating content where your community can actually talk back (gasp!).

Once you get over this sudden loss of control, you realize that this is an incredible opportunity to have an enriching conversation with your customers. It also means you can build deeper connections and relationships. And yet, according to data from the management consulting firm The Northridge Group, a full third (33 percent) of consumers who contact brands on social media never get a response.[4] That's because too many marketers continue to treat social media as they do traditional broadcast media. They talk—but they forget to listen.

Why is listening so hard? The answer is that most marketers are still spending more time and money on talking as opposed to listening. Back in Chapter 2, we discussed the perception gap between marketers and consumers, which showed that while 76 percent of marketers feel they know what their customers want, only 34 percent have bothered to ask them.[5] We'll get to asking questions in a moment, but first it's worth noting that there's so much you can learn by approaching your community in "listen-only mode."

Listen for the types of conversations that are taking place around your product and category. Listen to the conversations about your competitors from their customers and online detractors. Listen to the conversations found on their blog, podcast, and video comments. Above all, listen first. Listening is an easy step that can be applied by any organization, regardless of size or sector. What you learn will be invaluable and can help you plan your next steps.

Scrappy marketers don't always talk first. They listen and get their bearings. We're not done with listening just yet but as we start to talk, let's take a look at how questions can help us do more with less when it comes to digital marketing.

THE POWER OF QUESTIONS

How can we create more engaging conversations with our customers through social media? How can we develop more helpful content for our online community? These are both common questions for brands of all shapes and sizes. Guess what? You can actually answer these frequently asked questions *with* questions. That's because questions are currency when it comes to driving your social media and content marketing.

Whether you're trying to encourage conversations on your brand's Facebook page or create blog posts and videos that help your customers solve their problems, the best fuel for your digital marketing lies in the questions you ask and the questions your community asks. Why are questions so powerful? How about I illustrate this point with a question.

When I ask you a question, what do you have to do?

I'm guessing that, as you read that question, a response like "Answer it" popped into your head. Or perhaps you mumbled it to yourself. As best-selling author Daniel Pink notes in his book *To Sell Is Human*, the power of questions comes from the fact that they elicit an active response. "When I make a statement, you receive it passively," says Pink. "When I ask a question, you're compelled to respond, either aloud if the question is direct or silently if the question is rhetorical."[6]

Our innate social contract drives us to respond. As humans, we're hard-wired to answer questions. If we want to engage our community in social media conversations, questions are important building blocks. Answering questions also allows us to create helpful content for our customers. While helping customers solve problems is important at various stages of the sales cycle, it can have an even bigger impact on your long-term relationship with your customers.

Social psychologist and author Heidi Grant Halvorson notes that answering questions creates warmth, which in turn generates trust. "Asking questions makes the customer more likely to see you as warm—in other words, as someone who has good intentions toward them. This is one of the essential ingredients to establishing trust."[7]

Questions help us do more with less because they give us a smarter place to start in both our social media conversations and our content marketing. Instead of guessing at what matters most to your audience, use questions to spark social media conversations around topics of real interest. Instead of taking a stab at what kind of content you should create, ask your community what they need help with. As a marketer, you have to train yourself to see the value in questions. They are magical keys that allow you to unlock the power of doing more with less.

Let's take a look at how you can use questions to create a sustainable engine for your social media and content marketing.

HOW QUESTIONS FUEL CONTENT

Most marketers have an idea or two that gets them started with various forms of content. While that initial spark that gets your blog or podcast going is great, many marketers are stumped when it comes to sustaining these efforts. How can you create more posts that generate traffic and stand out in the increasingly noisy online marketplace? As mentioned in Chapter 3, Handley and Chapman remind us in *Content Rules* that the best content focuses on helping consumers solve their problems. Marketers should strive to "share or solve, not shill."[8] But how does one get started with all of this helping? The answer can be found in questions. Or, more specifically, in answering them.

As River Pools and Spa owner Marcus Sheridan has detailed in the *New York Times* and in stirring conference keynotes across the country, "answer[ing] all of the questions" was critical as he pulled his small business through one of the more challenging times in recent economic history. Swimming pools were pretty close to the top of the list of things people weren't buying at the height of the recent recession. Sheridan overcame this by poring over the search data in his category, where he found that there were thousands of questions around complex keyword combinations such as "fiberglass pool price" and "fiberglass pool quality." Armed with these questions—questions none of his competitors were addressing—he set about answering them all. In the end, he saved his business by creating what he now calls "The Most Educational Swimming Pool Blog in the Country"[9] (http://www.riverpoolsandspas.com/blog). Sheridan's work helped turn River Pools around, eventually earning a spot in the top 5 percent of U.S. in-ground pool sales.[10]

Questions can fuel long-form content like blog posts and white papers, but they can also provide idea-starters for short-form content as well. Lowe's uses questions as topics for their six-second Vine videos. Through their innovative "Fix in Six" campaign (https://vine.co/Lowes), the home improvement superstore answers customers' common and uncommon questions ("How do you get water stains off of your shower faucet? " "Looking to avoid bent bristles on your paint brushes?") with quick how-to videos. These small, simple doses of practical advice answer customer questions and build trust more effectively than just shooting videos of their featured products and end-cap displays.

Questions can take your content and your brand to surprising places. Mike Gerholdt used Salesforce's cloud-based customer relationship management (CRM) in roles at companies such as ACT, Inc., eventually becoming a certified administrator. In his spare time, he asked questions online to help him solve the problems he was encountering in the trenches. Recognizing that these answers could be useful to other "admins" out there, he created his blog ButtonClick Admin around the concept of "solving problems through clicks not code." In the end, Mike's content was such a valuable resource to the admin community at large that both he and his blog were acquired by Salesforce, where he continues to create helpful content for their community as an admin evangelist.

What questions do your customers have? How can you turn these potential pain points into useful content? You might be able to list these questions right off the top of your head; however, if you can't, don't worry. A quick discussion with your frontline team members in customer service or on the sales floor can usually yield a supply of several questions ready to be answered in your next blog post, podcast episode, or video series. For example, when I speak to business groups throughout the world, I use the Q & A session afterward as a means of gathering fuel for future content. If an audience member has a question based on something I'm talking about, there's a good chance others have that same question as well. That's why questions are great starting points for many forms of content.

Treat the questions your community asks as the currency they are by banking them. Use a straightforward idea-capture system such as a shared Google Doc or Evernote. You can get even scrappier by going old school and keeping a little notepad with you for questions (that's what I do for speaking engagements, workshops, and seminars). Just make sure you have some means of sharing these banked questions with the rest of your team. In doing so, you might help them recall useful questions they've heard. Your team is an invaluable resource in helping you brainstorm ideas and create content, as we'll discuss in the next chapter. More often than not, they're glad to help, but they need to know what you need from them in order to do so. Since questions are such a valuable part of your content marketing, ask your team to start gathering them for you.

As marketers, we're in the idea-capture business, as much of what we do depends on being able to retain the great content creation ideas we have. We need to further charge ourselves with being in the "question-capture business," in order to effectively capitalize on these digital idea starters. Answering questions helps you build the content that powers your online community. But it can also lead to more engaging social media conversations as well.

HOW QUESTIONS SPARK CONVERSATIONS

So, how can you make your next Facebook update or tweet more engaging? How can you post something that will ensure a like, comment, or retweet? Like content creation, the answer again lies in the question itself. In the case of social media, however, it lies in remembering to *ask questions* of your community as a means of getting them off the sidelines and involved in your brand's conversations online.

As Dave Kerpen notes in his book *Likeable Social Media*, posts that ask questions are nearly six times more engaging than those that don't.[11] What do you think someone is more likely to respond to, a post from a brand that merely states, "Happy Thanksgiving," or one that instead asks, "We're ready for turkey! What's *your* favorite Thanksgiving food?" This isn't a new concept. As marketers, we are constantly reminding ourselves to ask for the desired behavior with a clear call-to-action (CTA). Therefore, if we want to spark social media conversations we need to remember to ask for them. And the best way to ask for a conversation is through a question.

Questions can come in many forms. Beyond a traditional question, you can also prompt engagement with other question formats, including true/false, fill-in-the-blank, or click-to-like posts. Questions can be visual too, as Skinny Cow's Facebook page demonstrates. Fans of the Nestlé dessert brand are drawn in with an elaborate illustration of chocolate-covered wafers, nut clusters, and caramels floating above a desert island. The caption? "You're stranded on a desert island. Quick—which would you rather have?" The result? Thousands of likes, shares, and comments.

Michaels Stores, the craft and hobby-supply chain, uses their Instagram presence to ask visual questions such as "How is your creative space organized?" Michaels also employs questions in the visual content they share on social media. They ask questions to prompt engagement such as, "Still looking for the perfect Father's Day gift?" They then answer this question visually with a DIY idea, "Gather those cute kid pics and let them help make this portrait clock by #MichaelsMakers Make It and Love It for his office!"

Don't let the desserts and arts and crafts fool you. B2B companies can use questions to spark engagement among their customers as well. For example, Cisco frequently poses questions on their Facebook page such as, "Could smarter workplaces increase employee productivity, collaboration and overall happiness? Explore North America's smartest building and tell us what you think." This not only gets the audience thinking, it makes a point of asking for their input as well. Questions in all forms—whether simple text or amplified visually—provide triggers for customer responses.

In addition to sparking customer comments and conversations, you can get more prescriptive with what you ask your community to do. We'll talk more about encouraging user-generated content in Chapter 7; however, a simple request to your community can lead to an even greater level of engagement and deeper relationships over time. Moosejaw Mountaineering, highlighted in Chapter 3 for using social media "madness" to build a passionate community around their online and brick-and-mortar stores, gets scrappy with questions too.

With one simple question Moosejaw has transformed the task of keeping their Facebook cover photo updated into a fun opportunity for user-generated content. They have an ongoing request for "Custy Pics" (talk about brand voice!) on their Facebook page, which states, "We pick a new Moosejaw Custy Pic for our Cover Photo every week. You get a free tee (shirt) if we choose your pic. Post your pic on our wall or email them." The result contributes to their customer-focused brand story, while building up and rewarding their loyal and adventurous fans. Isn't that worth the price of a few t-shirts and shipping?

Rather than banking customer questions as discussed with content, with social media you need to remember to plot these questions on an editorial calendar to help plan your work. Forget the big tools and technology you're embarrassed about not having. A simple social media editorial calendar—it can literally be a paper calendar if it's easier for you and your team—is one of the scrappiest marketing tools out there.

Questions also bring us full circle as they can serve as great conclusions to your blog posts and other forms of content. If you want the content you create to start conversations, why don't you get things started with a question? There's no better way to encourage conversations and comments than by reaching into the therapist's bag of tricks and asking, "What do *you* think about that?" This too is an easy one to miss. As bloggers, we fall prey to traditional media constructs, which push us toward focusing on our own unidirectional broadcasts complete with a tidy conclusion that fails to invite the user to participate.

The end-with-a-question approach has long been heralded by Owner Media Group CEO and blogger Chris Brogan, who has one of the most engaging blogs on the social web. It's also a scrappy and blogger-friendly tactic as your conclusion essentially writes itself. *What do you think? How is your business approaching XYZ? We'd love to hear in the comments below.*

How will someone know to engage with you on social media or leave a comment on your content unless you ask them to do so?

TURNING A FEAR INTO OPPORTUNITY

One of the biggest fears around asking and answering questions online is that you won't always know the answer. For some, this is used as a reason to avoid the practice of asking questions entirely. *If we do this, someone is going to ask us a question we don't have the answer to!* While this is a normal fear, the response is disproportionate and prevents you from developing a marketing engine that will serve you well over time.

Getting over this requires a big admission for many brands: coming to terms with the fact that you won't always know the answer. As customer service experts know, it's okay to acknowledge that you don't have all of the answers. However, we marketers have long been under the impression that we have complete control over building our brand and should always have a perfect and well-crafted response to any question. As discussed earlier, our communications aren't one-way anymore. The audience talks back now and frequently asks questions. And in many cases, they are questions we don't have perfect answers for. Yet.

Once you get over this fear, you realize the opportunity that being open to these questions presents. There could be new forms of content you could create to answer these new questions. It could be a new topic of conversation on your various social channels. As cartoonist and author James Thurber famously said, "It is better to know some of the questions than all of the answers." The value of seeking "the questions" outweighs boorishly asserting that you'll always have all of the answers.

Not always knowing is okay as it can provide further direction on how you can serve your community even better down the road.

- - - - - - - - - - - -
AFTER THE QUESTION:
LISTENING AND RESPONDING

Remember how we said we'd get back to listening? Even with our question engine powering our conversations and content, our work isn't done. Digital marketing is defined by the fact that it is multidirectional as opposed to a one-way blast of information at your audience. If correctly developed, your marketing will spark conversations. This means you need to continue to actively listen. You can't just "wait to talk," ignoring what others might be adding.

You can't just listen; you have to be *seen* as listening. If you think back to any basic speech or communications class, you'll recall that it's important to give verbal and nonverbal cues when someone else is speaking—nodding your head, quietly saying "mm hmm," "uh-huh," and so forth. These active listening cues can be challenging when it comes to social media. Here are a few ways to show that you are listening across various digital channels.

Simply remembering to ask for engagement can be useful when managing your communities on Facebook, Twitter, and LinkedIn. We've established that questions can serve as effective icebreakers for community managers looking to ignite conversation among their followers. This is where the opportunity for active listening begins.

Once the question is asked, many marketers sit back and let the answers roll in instead of showing that they are listening. Just as you would nod along with a speaker who is talking to you, you should also look for ways to show your online speakers that you are listening as well. At the most basic level, consider liking or favoriting each new comment from a community member. If it's at all complimentary, a simple "thank you" can go a long way toward showing someone that you care.

If this sounds like a massive undertaking, consider the Humane Society of the United States, which works to respond to each and every comment on their Facebook page—an audience of over a million people. "It is our policy to answer every legitimate question or concern that comes to us via one of our social media channels, and in a timely manner," explains Carie Lewis Carlson, deputy director of online communications at the Humane Society of the United States.

"This is so important because people come to social media for interaction; if they just wanted to read about what you're doing, they'd go to your website."[12] In the end, a 1:1 listening and engagement strategy—where you respond to each and every comment—is a good rule of thumb.

In Dove's most recent addition to their long-term "Campaign for Real Beauty," they use social media to post inspiring quotes, share touching videos, and ask engaging questions of their followers. A brand this emotionally involved can't simply ask these questions and leave the responses up there with no reaction. That's why Dove makes an effort to respond in a positive and affirming brand voice to each response they receive.

Good comments aren't the only ones that merit active listening. If someone is upset at your brand and voices a concern on social media, often the first step toward mending their issue is simply speaking up and stating that you're here and you're listening to them, as in my experience with the New Pioneer Food Co-op shared earlier. Even if it's something that you need to pass along to another department for resolution, embracing the person who posted the comment quickly with a message of care shows that your brand is listening.

You'll notice that listening bookends our question engine. You have to listen first to know what kind of questions you can ask and answer. If you've done your job effectively, you need to continue this listening for the conversations and comments that follow. As the digital channel is different and void of traditional forms of supportive listening cues, you need to work to show that you are, in fact, listening. If all of this sounds a lot like relationship advice, it's because that's what this really is—building closer, more human relationships online.

GETTING YOUR TEAM ENGAGED

As we'll discuss in the next chapter, getting your team off of the bench and into the game is another critical step in doing more with less and getting scrappy with your marketing. As mentioned earlier in this chapter, in many cases your team will be eager to help. However, they need to understand what it is you need help with. That's another benefit to thinking of your marketing strategy as a map. When you're on a road trip, it's easy to pass a map to the backseat so others can see where you're going and even assist you with the navigation. Because listening and questions are critical components in getting scrappy with social media conversations and content, let's take a look at a couple of ideas for involving your team in capturing these resources.

As a means of keeping management and the rest of your team informed, consider creating an easy-to-share listening report featuring the top posts that were commented upon, customer feedback and questions, and maybe something fun. Make this your regular contribution to meetings when it's time for you to share an update. Use these reports as conversation starters on how your team can be more involved in your organization's marketing.

Another idea that starts with better internal communications is making sure everyone understands that questions are currency when it comes to your marketing. Use your listening report as a means of opening a dialogue on what questions you can ask and answer online. This is also a perfect opportunity for soliciting questions from frontline areas in your organization such as sales and customer service. You can consider sharing access to your question bank on Google Docs, Evernote, or Basecamp so that others can contribute. If employee engagement is slow going, consider some fun prizes or maybe contributions to your organization's favorite charity when you hit a certain threshold of employee participation or number of questions in your bank.

We'll discuss this more in the following chapter, but clearly communicating the mechanics of your digital marketing engine, what you value (questions, listening), and more will help your team understand how they can be a more active part of your marketing, helping you do more with less. Like questions, your team is an invaluable and often underutilized resource in overcoming the Myth of Big.

 **NEXT STEPS**

Listening to your customers, asking questions, and listening to the answers you receive must be a bigger part of your marketing. Answering the questions below will get you started on the right path.

- What does your audience need help with? How can you answer those questions through your content?

- What kinds of questions can you ask your audience? Brainstorm 10 ideas right now. They may be more valuable than you think.

- Are you asking questions at the end of your content to spark ongoing comments and conversations?

- What kind of a system can you create for your team to help you keep track of customer questions that you can use to spark social media conversations and create helpful content?

- How can you and your team utilize an editorial calendar to plan your social media and content marketing?

— Can you institute an activity with your team where you regularly share the most interesting (jaw-dropping, surprising, best, worst) insight from one of your customers or community members?

Chapter 5

EMBRACE YOUR PEOPLE POWER

So we need to be listening online? Yes. *We need to be gathering customer questions?* Uh-huh. *Then we use all of these questions to create a lot of content like blog posts and videos?* Correct. *And then we use all of these topics to start social media conversations?* Affirmative. *And this content and social media all lives online and is happening 24 hours a day, 7 days a week, 365 days of the year?!?* Yep.

If these panicked thoughts were rushing through your head, take comfort in the fact that you're not alone. One resource marketers aren't short on today is frustration. We have a lot to do! And, as Schwinn's Samantha Hersil reminded us earlier, we could all do with a few more people and a few dollars more.[1]

However, like the mousetrap, we have to create marketing that is more effective and efficient than ever before. To do this, we're going to need some help.

When we start talking about social media and our people, we're quick to point out all of our "people problems"—people wasting time, not having the right people, not having enough people, and so on. The Myth of Big also complicates our relationship with our people. *Only big brands with big teams, big tools, and big technology can do big things.* While there may be some general correlation between the size of an organization and the size of its marketing team, there are several marketers doing great things who don't have big teams at all. They've decided to get scrappy instead.

Our challenge is one part myth-busting the issues that complicate getting our people more involved in our digital marketing. It's also one part understanding how to get scrappy with our staffing. As Jay Baer notes in his best-selling book *Youtility,* "Your employees are your single greatest marketing engine."[2] In the end, you shouldn't have a people *problem.* By getting scrappy, you can learn to embrace your people *power* and do more than you could have ever imagined with less.

But first we need to shatter some myths. In most organizations, the biggest concerns related to people and digital marketing come down to three core issues: time, talent, and terror.

TIME: THE REAL PEOPLE PROBLEM

Make no mistake about it, for many, there is a people problem in marketing today. "Lack of time" is among the biggest content marketing challenges reported across industries, according to the Content Marketing Institute and MarketingProfs.[3] This lack of time is directly associated with who's doing the work and how it's getting done. Data from Salesforce shows that 60 percent of organizations have a 1- to 3-person social media team.[4] Complicating this even further is the fact that these individuals often have other roles internally. "We don't have enough people" or "Our people don't have enough time" are comments frequently heard in the corridors of businesses big and small.

We're also concerned with other personnel issues related to social media. "I don't want my people on Facebook all day!" is another common complaint. This myth is easy to debunk with a quick trip down memory lane (this will date me). Remember when we were scared of employees wasting time if we provided them with access to email? Or the fear that if employees had phones at their desks they would make a lot of long-distance phone calls? (Young people reading this: Don't laugh, these were actual concerns before we all had phones *with* email in our pockets.) Social media and mobile technology are simply the latest generation of business tools. To embrace our people power online, we can't get tangled up in fears of how our people will waste time. (For what it's worth, in most cases a time-wasting employee is usually wasting time in other areas, not just social media.)

The big question is, what are we going to do about these obstacles if we want to do more with less? Few organizations are looking to add head count these days, especially in marketing, where we continue to see annual budgets directed toward tools and technology purchases rather than additional staff. Instead of getting frustrated with this reality, we need to focus on getting scrappy with our staffing and how we allocate time. Before we look at some models for using our time more effectively, let's debunk another people myth related to our team's talent.

TALENT: SOCIAL MEDIA UNICORNS DON'T EXIST

A convenient excuse for organizations looking for a reason *not* to rethink their marketing is the objection that "We don't have the right employees to do something like that." Maybe this thinking is a result of the bumper crop of Internet-famous marketing gurus we now have due in large part to social media. Or perhaps it's the news media's intense focus on how different marketing today is, as opposed to my central thesis that, while the megaphone has changed, the core principles underlying our efforts—brand building, sound strategy, meaningful metrics—remain solid.

Whether marketing has changed radically or remains essentially the same, a stereotype has certainly developed of what a digital marketer is, creating a difficult and unrealistic benchmark for internal staff to live up to. I call this stereotype "the social media unicorn." These individuals are just as mythical as the creatures whose name I've co-opted. Sometimes the search for social media unicorns masks a thinly veiled ageism. Organizations looking to hire digital natives to staff up their new marketing efforts are missing the boat. As Mirum President Mitch Joel wryly asserts in his book *Ctrl Alt Delete* on the subject of digital natives, "You may plug in a lot of stuff, but that doesn't make you an electrician."[5] There's no correlation between effective digital marketing and the age of one's team.

Organizations taking their marketing to the next level are executing integrated campaigns with strategies and tactics tied back to measurable business goals. A study from Altimeter Group shows that most successful social media marketers have at least three to six years' experience in digital marketing and have multidisciplinary backgrounds. Actual "experience with social media" ranked fifth on the list of skills behind key organizational talents such as being "multidisciplinary," "wearing many hats," and "willing to take risks."[6]

Similar data ranking skills provided by the Community Management Roundtable put engagement and people skills, content development skills, and strategic and business skills ahead of technical skills.[7] The biggest pitfall for marketers is this deep yet erroneous belief that social media is some kind of mysterious hieroglyphics that can only be decoded by youth with a special set of technical skills.

Instead of chasing these unicorns we need to stop making excuses and review our own bench of internal talent for those who have led successful initiatives, can get buy-in throughout the organization, and who understand interpersonal customer engagement.

Social media is a marketing channel that can be used for great things, whether it's global brands like Ford launching new products or local brands like New Pioneer Co-op delivering exceptional customer service (FYI: At the time of this writing, both companies are led by marketers over the age of 25 who are doing phenomenal things in spite of this impairment). These are complex business strategies requiring marketing experience, not simply a birth certificate with the right date stamp. My daughter is a digital native who has navigated iOS since she was three but that doesn't mean you should hire her as an app developer.

Beyond ageism, another breed of social media unicorn can rear its head under the false pretense that you're putting your brains before budget. We've all heard it before. Or you may have actually said it yourself. "Let's have the intern get us started on social media." Entrusting the launch of your brand on a new platform solely to an intern is troublesome for a variety of reasons. Perhaps the biggest one is the same step most miss in developing a digital marketing strategy—establishing clear and measurable business objectives. As a marketer, you need to put on your big boy/big girl pants and tackle this issue head on and in-house instead of farming it out to an intern.

While interns alone shouldn't be responsible for mapping your marketing strategy, they can certainly help out as you head down the path. Working with your organization's marketing leaders, your intern can both learn more about your business and apply his or her social media insights as a digital native to your objectives. Armed with your vision of what your business needs are, your intern may be able to point you to a new Facebook feature or help you understand emerging platforms. Your interns can also help you out tactically.

With guidance on your strategy and a firm grasp of your brand's voice, an intern can help execute your social media presence—after all, you can't send every tweet yourself. Plus, an intern can be a useful "floater" as you evaluate your long-term staff resources.

Ultimately, the concern that you don't have the right people is another obstacle in disguise. In many cases, we stereotype the social media unicorns to mask the fact that we don't know what we're doing with our digital marketing. As such, we have no idea what kind of help we need. This is where the smart steps we took in Part One— developing your brand blueprint, mapping your marketing, and following your digital compass—should help us know exactly what skill sets we need for reimagining marketing. If you're launching a social customer service initiative, you need some enhanced social media training for your existing call-center staff. If you're building your brand through expert content, you need to teach some of your marketing managers and copywriters new skills that will enable them to become content creators and thought leaders.

As we'll continue to discuss, your people should not be viewed as a problem, as they are a critical component of your success.

TERROR: LIVING WITH DIGITAL CHAOS

The final internal obstacle is terror. Wide-eyed, white-knuckled terror at how all of this potentially changes one of the most complex aspects of our organization—our people. Anything involving personnel is scary, whether you're a small business adding your first full-time employee or a Fortune 500 staring down a reorganization. These decisions usually are slow and cumbersome, depending on culture and leadership. They take time, consideration, and careful planning. *And now you're doing the same thing to our marketing!?!*

With the rise of social media and digital marketing, everyone on your team now has the potential to be a brand ambassador. But what does this mean operationally? *If my employees are hourly, do I need to pay them for after-hours engagement? What about the fact that we are telling them that Facebook is a big part of our marketing, but we've blocked it on our internal network? Speaking of which, what about our employee policy?*

Make no mistake, this can be scary stuff. Largely because it represents a loss of control. However, marketing today is defined by a shift in control, as consumers can talk back to us, which in turn provides us with the opportunity to build close relationships. This is very different and does involve ceding some control. As the marketing leader and internal change agent, it's up to you to help bring these issues to the surface early on so no one is surprised down the road.

Remember how the Altimeter data said that successful social media marketers were good at rallying support internally?[8] This is the application for that very critical skill. You'll need to work with the appropriate teams internally, educating them on what you're trying to do, why it's important, and what you've seen work throughout your industry and from studying best practices.

Time, talent, and terror concerns are all opportunities for you to build trust internally. One of the best ways you can build trust is by assuring them that you have a scrappy plan for dividing and conquering the new work that lies ahead.

DIVIDING AND CONQUERING

To get scrappy with your staffing, you first have to understand who is doing what. To do that, you have to get RACI with your staffing. Not to be confused with the HR nightmare that would be "racy staffing," you need to breakdown your digital roles and responsibilities using this model, which proves especially useful in tying together the scrappy cross-functional teams you'll need to embrace your people power.

A RACI staffing plan for your marketing efforts means that you have identified who is:

— *Responsible:* These are the individuals working with you responsible for specific tasks along the way. These could be freelance writers creating blog content, a video resource, or your customer service team monitoring your Twitter feed for support issues. Sometimes this is you, if you are responsible for completing specific tasks.

— *Accountable:* If you're reading this, there's a pretty good chance that this is you and you alone. There can be only one person accountable for a plan and you're it. It's okay if you want to run. Take a deep breath. As the accountable party, you are also the one who approves work from those responsible on your team.

— *Consulted:* Those you consult with such as subject matter experts. If you are preparing blog content about your product, you might need to consult your engineering staff. If you have an organizational question, you might consult management. Communication at this level is two-way.

— *Informed:* Those you keep informed and in the loop on what you're up to as a general FYI. For example, after establishing a clear plan beforehand, you'll want to keep other departments like HR, IT, and legal informed of progress on your new initiatives.

Now that you know who your players are on the field, who's calling the plays, and who's advising from up in the booth—a football metaphor can be helpful here—it's time to look at how we organize our teams. Data from Altimeter Group also shows us that most organizations employ a hub-and-spoke approach with a centralized cross-functional digital marketing node helping various business units.[9]

In many cases, that digital hub internally will be you. If you're lucky, it may be you and a few members of your trusted team. Regardless, you're the one who is accountable. Based on your destination and compass coordinates established in Chapters 2 and 3, you'll need to identify your responsible parties and others who you'll need to consult and inform along the way. Again, if your mission is focused on content detailing the inner workings of your industry and products, then you'll need to consult your internal experts on the product team. If your initiative is focused on customer service, you may need to keep your operations or logistics team informed on issues arising on your brand's Facebook page and new resolutions that may be coming down the pike.

With an idea of how we can organize our teams, let's look at how to apply this with some examples of companies getting scrappy with their staffing both internally and externally.

INTERNAL SCRAPPY STAFFING

When it comes to how the work is done, you need to encourage some flexibility among yourself and your team. Our linear way of thinking about roles and responsibilities isn't the best fit for the new world of marketing, which is fragmented and requires a variety of skill sets. That's why many scrappy marketers have found success sharing the work internally.

One of my favorite examples for debunking the Myth of Big is Ben & Jerry's, the very definition of a global brand. With product sold worldwide, there is always a Ben & Jerry's scoop shop that is open or a store where you can buy your Cherry Garcia or Half Baked. Given their corporate footprint, it's easy to assume that the Vermont-based ice cream maker would simply throw people at this challenge. However, their own internal team handling their digital marketing efforts takes a decidedly scrappy approach.

"We have an interesting setup where we have a few different community managers," says Mike Hayes, Ben & Jerry's digital marketing manager. "One of our web development team members manages our Twitter account. Our associate brand manager manages our Facebook account. I, as the digital marketing manager, manage all of the emerging platforms and also oversee strategy for all of the networks."[10] It's hard to imagine what this would look like on an org chart, especially an org chart for a company of their size.

What can you learn from Ben & Jerry's staffing? It's easy to get siloed in our organizations, regardless of size. Don't let departmental barriers hold you up. If a customer service rep has a lot of experience engaging on a social network where you're about to launch a presence, consider making them the lead or *responsible* party under the RACI model. Your new scrappy marketing team will be much more cross-functional and dynamic. And they may not all sit in the marketing department. Learn to embrace the chaos of a flatter org chart with a few extra dotted lines where individuals can cross over and help.

You might also benefit from dividing up the work based on complexity or urgency. Pancheros Mexican Grill is a chain of fast-casual Tex-Mex restaurants that serve Mexican-style cuisine throughout the United States with an emphasis on burrito-loving college towns in the Midwest. Though they have over 60 locations, their marketing staff consists of two marketers—a director of marketing and a local-store marketer ("local-store marketer" is their job title for the junior member of the marketing team). They divide the work up based on complexity and urgency.

"Our local-store marketer is responsible for the fun aspect of our social media in a lot of ways," says Reid Travis, director of marketing communications for Pancheros and social media lead. "I respond mostly to complaints, concerns, and more serious customer interactions."[11] In short, basic engagement happens via junior staff while key issues are escalated to the team leader.

What can you learn from Pancheros' staffing? Don't get hung up on the number of people you have. Instead, look for creative ways to divide up the work, such as the level of engagement (basic vs. complex issues, urgency, etc.).

Another scrappy staffing example is New Belgium Brewing, which was mentioned in Chapter 2 for their innovative approach to community building using Facebook and Twitter. (More on that in a bit.) They also use Instagram as a social media channel. With one of the larger followings in the craft-brewing category, one might assume that New Belgium employs a large team to support these efforts. However, their strategy is decidedly scrappy.

New Belgium started by job-sharing management of the social network, meaning that five employees kept their Instagram photos updated but it wasn't anyone's full time job. Over time, this strategy has evolved even further. Today New Belgium has one centrally located employee responsible for several social media channels. This team member relies on regular content contributions from their local marketing team members. "Our field marketers generate good content on a regular basis, so when we see a post we know will resonate nationally, we grab it and post from the main account. Not only does it ease the workload of our digital team, it helps grow the local field marketer's Instagram following," said Kevin Darst, New Belgium's digital manager.[12] It's also a scrappy way of dividing and conquering the digital duties.

What can you learn from New Belgium's staffing? This is a classic example of scrappy staffing and a good reminder to see ideas everywhere. Regardless of your business, who couldn't employ an approach like this? Consider dividing responsibility for individual networks or content tasks like blogging across several employees. Beyond being efficient, this can add variety to your content and conversations, as Darst notes.

There are so many new forms of marketing, it's not practical to simply add a new person every time you launch a new social network or undertake a new form of content. Look for ways you can utilize overlapping skill sets across various forms of media. After looking at getting scrappy internally, how might we embrace our people power outside our walls?

EXTERNAL SCRAPPY STAFFING

Sometimes being scrappy with your staffing means not everything can get done inside your company's four walls. There are a few core groups that can come to your aid. First, consider employees working in the field. A good segue from looking at scrappy internal staffing to sharing your work externally is provided (again!) by New Belgium Brewing. As we learned in Chapter 2, the company has Instagram and Twitter pages in key markets across the country. But remember, they aren't managed by internal staff. Members of their team support these efforts with product news and updates, but ultimately provide latitude to each "field marketer" in specific markets to add local flavor to their social presence.

Another cost-effective group to consider are your raving fans. Patagonia empowers their community to be a part of their marketing as well. The socially responsible California-based clothing company encourages fans to share the stories behind their favorite garments on their Worn Wear blog. Given Patagonia's focus on clothing and gear for adventurous pursuits such as skiing, surfing, and climbing, these personal testimonies are a mix of motivation and emotion. "Patagonia runs in our family," says a post from Halley Roberts of Santa Fe, New Mexico. "I remember being held as a small kid next to the soft fabric of my dad's Synchilla Fleece that he still wears."[13] Content like this passes the test of being both effective and efficient. It tells the brand's story in a compelling and cost-efficient way and furthers the customers' ownership, both of the site and of the product.

We'll take a closer look at how you can engage your happy customers as brand ambassadors and foster user-generated content in Chapter 7.

The next group to consider are your external agency resources. Getting scrappy with staffing can be beneficial to agencies and marketing services firms that understand this mindset and the call to be effective and efficient. Previously, agencies were used to owning every piece of a project or campaign. As social media has democratized marketing communications, these responsibilities have diffused and agency roles continue to evolve. As agencies get scrappy with their own staffing, filling their benches with in-house digital "A-Teams," you can find interesting and mutually beneficial partnerships beyond the traditionally defined agency-client relationship.

For example, a core competency of many agencies is media buying. In the past this meant placing television, radio, print, and outdoor ads. Today, many agencies are applying these media-buying capabilities to paid search and social advertising on platforms such as

Google, Facebook, Twitter, and more. Additionally, as we see from Edison data, customers continue to engage online after hours—outside the regular business day.[14] As a result, many businesses struggle to continue listening and engaging after hours. In some cases, agency teams can serve as the digital "third shift" by providing monitoring services on nights and weekends and identifying any emergencies that may arise.

Agencies can also add external bandwidth to internal team members who are often wearing many hats. As both the senior vice president for executive communications and chief marketing officer, Tamsen Webster literally wears two hats at Oratium, a messaging consultancy. Charged with creating expert content for the firm's blog, she struggled to find time to get her ideas out of her head and into posts. SHIFT Communications, Oratium's agency partner, had a scrappy idea for getting this done. The SHIFT team would interview Webster and then draft blog posts based on these conversations, which she in turn would edit. "It's a massive time-saver for us as a team, and for me personally," said Webster. "I can speak for days, but have a mental block against writing. Having SHIFT interview us and then write kills multiple birds with one stone."[15]

As social networks like Instagram, Pinterest, and Snapchat continue to get more visual, agencies can continue to do what they've always done. Provide bold, attention-getting creative ideas to help clients stand out. In fact, the Lowe's "Fix in Six" Vine campaign referenced earlier was developed by their agency partners at BBDO.

While internal teams may be able to create content and engage more effectively on social networks because they are so much closer to their product or organization, outside agencies, consultants, and freelancers can offer complementary skills and increased bandwidth. A scrappy combination of an internal team member and an outside agency resource can serve as an effective, efficient pairing.

------- -

CASE STUDIES,
COMMAND CENTERS, AND TOOLS

As we wrap up our review of how we can get scrappy with our staffing and implementation, let's debunk a few final myths. First, as I've suggested many times throughout this book, you need to have the courage to look beyond your industry. It's easy to read case studies featuring similar businesses, in search of something to mirror; it's comforting to parrot back what a company in your category has already done. However, this approach is less than ideal for a couple of reasons. For starters, there could be additional factors that made a particular strategy work for them but may hinder things for you. Furthermore, like any copycat, you'll be an echo instead of the original. When you sift through ideas from everywhere, you get an added layer of originality and freshness. Plus, if you borrow an operational tactic such as New Belgium's Instagram job-sharing, it's simply a means to an end that still serves your unique goals.

Another approach we see overblown in case studies and other forms of media is that of the social media command center. It's not hard to find stories online of brands implementing a NASA-like mission control center for their social media that they in turn show off to the news media. It could seem to many that this bigger physical space with bigger tools (the screens—oh the screens!) is a necessity as you scale up your marketing. While there are times when a command center makes sense—like for the Red Cross during disasters or for the NFL during the weeks leading up to the Super Bowl—often there's more sizzle than steak to these stories. A scrappy marketer does more with less across the board, including physical space. Unless having a command center accomplishes some unique aspect of your organization's objectives or map, ignore the hype around bigger, cooler spaces.

At this point you might be wondering if this chapter will cover any of the tools and technology that you can use to make your marketing more effective and efficient. The short answer is no. While there are a number of useful tools you can employ, the intention of this book is to create a scrappy framework to help you organize your marketing and the people who will help you bring it to life. An in-depth discussion of specific platforms that help us manage and measure our efforts would be fruitless, because they evolve almost as quickly as the channels themselves.

What's more relevant to our framework is that most organizations are getting scrappy with their tools as well. Instead of committing to massive one-stop solutions, most marketers are using a combination of free and paid tools.[16] Here again it's easy to get caught up in the Myth of Big. Like the command center concept, bigger tools and technology won't significantly impact your marketing as much as having a solid strategic foundation will.

To be clear, there are several great tools available made by whip-smart marketers such as HootSuite, HubSpot, and Salesforce. Many can help you and your team realize efficiencies such as scheduling posts, monitoring, measurement, and more. But don't get lost among the Shiny New Things here, either. Define your plan and find the best tools to help your team follow your map and reach your destination.

- - - - - - - - - - - - - - - - -
YOUR MOST VALUABLE RESOURCE

As you consider how to embrace your people power, it's important not to lose sight of the process point made at the end of the last chapter. If you want your team to be a part of your marketing, it's your responsibility to bring them up to speed on your plan and, most importantly, ask them for what you need. If you don't know exactly what you need or how they might be able to help, consider a mainstay approach of parent/teacher organizations and other volunteer-driven groups and distribute an internal time-and-talent form to learn more about what others are interested in, what skills they have, and what they can do for you. This could be your first step in learning that a team member might be an unexpected source for blog posts or photos because of their personal passion for writing or photography that may not be shining through in their current responsibilities.

By engaging your employees, you're also creating an asset that can aid you in the event of a future crisis. That's because socially active and engaged teams are more likely to rise to your defense should you make a misstep or have a misunderstanding within your community. During the 2013 holiday season, a sharp uptick in online shopping coupled with crippling ice storms resulted in UPS getting behind in their deliveries. This enraged many gift-givers, who took to social media to complain. Without being prompted, drivers like Larry Ledet stepped forward in defense of the brand as he shared his story of his 60-hour workweek and wished followers a Merry Christmas. While many customers shared their own missed delivery stories and continued to attack, his comment generated 917 likes and 145 replies, with many expressing appreciation for his work. UPS's social media team responded to many of the comments, but they also took a minute to thank Ledet for his service to the company.[17]

Your people are your most precious resource. How you cultivate this resource is through your culture. "Culture is everything," notes consultant, author, and speaker Mark W. Schaefer, who has worked with organizations as diverse as Adidas, Johnson & Johnson, and the U.S. Air Force. When I interviewed Schaefer about what most are missing organizationally when it comes to social media, he quickly noted, "Culture is the number one predictor of success. Not budget, not resources." In citing his work with Dell, he added, "Their success was because the person at the top got it."[18]

You must develop a culture that embraces social media at your organization. Your marketing doesn't stand a chance without cultural support from employees as well as your organization's leaders. Start by simply letting employees know it's okay to access social media at work. From there, you can invite them to share relevant company updates with their friends and followers online.

Remember, as human as our new marketing channels are, you cannot allow people to be the problem. Happy employees create happy customers, who we'll talk more about in the chapters ahead. By embracing your people power internally and externally, you'll have taken a big step toward getting scrappy and doing more with less.

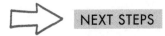 **NEXT STEPS**

Start embracing your people power by answering the questions below.

— What are your biggest internal obstacles to embracing your people power? Take a moment and sketch out your concerns related to each of the following (acknowledging your obstacles is big step toward resolving them):

- Time

- Talent

- Terror

— How can you get scrappy with your internal staffing? Can you divide and conquer based on social network? Or can you split things up based on complexity and/or urgency?

- Are there ways you can get scrappy externally? How can you encourage your fans to help you create content? Are there skills your agency partners bring to the table?

- Forget the social media command center. What kind of physical space does your team actually need?

- Consider your marketing map from Chapter 2 and the compass points plotted in Chapter 3. What tools and technology are needed to support these efforts?

- How can you foster a culture that embraces your organization's people power?

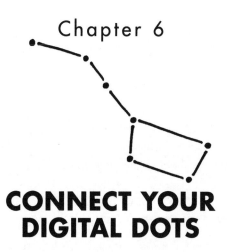

Chapter 6

CONNECT YOUR DIGITAL DOTS

If you stand too close to the painting *A Sunday Afternoon on the Island of La Grande Jatte* by French impressionist Georges Seurat, you don't see much of anything at all. It just looks like a series of dots scattered across a canvas. As you step back, the whole comes into focus as the sum of all of the parts. Through his pointillism technique, Seurat created a science of color and light among these dots, which your eyes ultimately connect. View these microscopic elements independently and they aren't remarkable at all. View them in concert with one another and you have a work of art.

These dots are similar to your individual digital marketing efforts—social media and content marketing as well as your other channels including paid search, organic search, email marketing, and, of course, your website. As fragmented as our attention is today, it's very easy to accidentally end up with fragmented digital marketing. While you can't say that these individual channels aren't effective on their own, like Seurat's dots they aren't nearly as powerful as they can be once they're connected.

Bringing all of these points together helps us to market like a

- - -

mousetrap—getting effective and efficient by connecting our digital dots. Like embracing the power of questions and people, bringing these channels together helps us do more with less. As Steve Jobs famously said abut Apple's ability to create innovative products, "Creativity is just connecting things." As marketers we need to get better at connecting things if we want to get scrappy.

This too is easier said than done. The payoff can be considerable, but how do you go about connecting the dots in your marketing?

OBSESS OVER DIGITAL INTEGRATION

You have to get obsessive about digital integration. Indeed, many marketers are already obsessed with integration. Recent data from both Altimeter Group and CMO Survey shows that better integration across marketing platforms is consistently one of the top areas of concern and additional investment for marketers.[1]

Better integration among our digital marketing channels helps us further maximize our effectiveness and efficiency. An integrated marketing campaign stands a better chance of being effective if each component in the mix has been planned with the rigor outlined in Chapters 2 and 3—mapping your marketing strategy and following your digital compass—with any of your digital channels. When each channel has a map defined by a unique destination or business objective, they can all work toward accomplishing these goals and can complement one another to cover even more ground. As with the Seurat painting, the whole is greater than the sum of its parts.

When these parts are planned and executed in concert, it's also easier to realize efficiencies among your efforts. For example, your content marketing may consist of several regular blog posts and videos. This content could be easily repurposed in your email marketing efforts. If it's on point for your content marketing map and destination, it should align with your email strategy as well (and vice versa). The potential savings come into play when you consider the internal time or external expense of creating additional content for both your content marketing and your email marketing. By connecting your digital dots, you reinforce your message and save money. You can do more with less.

As we expand our efforts to include social media and content marketing in addition to the tried-and-true components of our digital marketing mix—email, search, website—it's easy to oversimplify social media integration to just mean slapping the Facebook and Twitter logos on our websites and emails. While this is an elementary step, there's much more to be done when it comes to real digital marketing integration.

TAKE YOUR SOCIAL MEDIA INTEGRATION TO THE NEXT LEVEL

Social media icons are ubiquitous as we traverse the online and offline marketplace. Whenever I see them standing alone on a website masthead or on a sign or a banner accompanied by the request to "Follow Us," I shake my head and silently ask the brand, "Why should I follow you?"

Because these icons have become such an easy way to define integration, many think nothing more of it. Sometimes this is simply a missed opportunity, as there really are compelling reasons why a customer should follow you. (Special savings? Exclusive offers? Expert tips?) However, sometimes this is a symptom of an even bigger disease touched on just a few times in this book—the lack of a clear strategy.

As scrappy marketers we need to remember not to get lost in "the sizzle" of social channels and instead focus our attention on "the steak"—the basic tenets of strong direct marketing. When inviting people to connect with your brand on Facebook, Twitter, Instagram, and other networks—an action you want them to take—you need to sweeten the deal. You know why you want them to follow you, but *they* don't yet know what's in it for them and they need to know if you want them to take that next step. You need to create a strong call to action that leads with a benefit to the consumer.

- *Get the latest news* by connecting with us on Twitter

- Like us on Facebook for *special offers and exclusive savings*

- *Help us shape new product development* on our LinkedIn group

This may sound trivial, but it's definitely not. These frontline brand touch points are what transform your casual traffic—both online and off—into members of your community, closer to your inner circle, where you can communicate with them more consistently and personally. With each step closer to that inner circle, they're also closer to becoming customers and, if you can keep them engaged, brand advocates and ambassadors for life.

Connecting your digital dots is so much more than ensuring that you've got social media icons on the rest of your marketing. Let's take a look at some of the best strategies for connecting your marketing to make it more efficient and effective.

WHY EMAIL MARKETING STILL MATTERS

If you really pry, you can often get marketers to admit to a guilty pleasure. They like email marketing. Yet too often we hear the following . . . *Email?!? Not email! For starters, email has nothing to do with any of the Shiny New Things. Plus, we've been talking about email for decades now. Decades! With an* s*! Does email still matter?*

While this might be a bit of an overstatement, email is definitely treated as a black sheep among the social media set. We spend tons of time on blogs, chats, and at conferences dissecting the minutia of the most recent Pinterest and Snapchat data (*What does it mean? Can it really mean that??*) and much less time talking about one of the oldest forms of social media. And yet, email is stronger than ever and producing results in a big way.

Sarahjane Sacchetti, who helps market start-ups, bravely made this admission during her South by Southwest (SXSW) panel on social media: "While all marketers love to talk about the newest, coolest platforms and tactics, we're less excited to brag about our latest email marketing campaign. Well, here's the thing. It's measurable. It works. It may not be sexy, but it's still incredibly powerful."[2] And the results are getting stronger with each passing year.

Here are the cold, hard facts about email marketing:

- **Channel Performance:** MailerMailer's annual Email Marketing Metrics Report reveals that open rates are up year after year.[3]

- **Purchase Influence:** According to ExactTarget, email still leads the pack when it comes to influencing buying decisions.[4]

- **Return on Investment:** The Direct Marketing Association (DMA) reports that email marketing has an ROI of 4,000 percent.[5] eConsultancy reports that 72 percent of email marketers call their ROI excellent or good.[6]

- **Budget Allocation:** StrongView showed that 61 percent of marketers plan on increasing their email marketing budgets, ahead of both social media and mobile.[7]

Some Shiny New Things don't fare as well when compared to email. For example, a recent Ipsos survey noted that 75 percent of consumers preferred to have brands or stores send their promotions to their email in-box rather than using Short Message Service (SMS) or text messaging, a shiny new channel that marketers wrongly think customers want to receive more marketing on.[8] The in-box is a very special place to be granted access to. Most texts still feel like interruptions. You check email when you want to. And you've given your permission to the brands that you want to be in there.

Email marketing remains an effective tool as it allows for targeted, data-driven marketing while also building loyalty, trust, and a strong brand over time through consistent communications. But how can we better connect our email with our new digital marketing efforts?

HOW TO INTEGRATE EMAIL WITH YOUR SOCIAL MEDIA AND CONTENT MARKETING

DJ Waldow, coauthor of *The Rebel's Guide to Email Marketing*, is fond of saying that email and social media marketing go together like Batman and Robin. "How many of you have checked your email in the past week? How about the past 24 hours? The past hour? Since you've been reading this? Email is ingrained into our daily lives," notes Waldow. "Yes, people spend an inordinate amount of time on social media sites like Facebook and Twitter, but email has been—and always will be—the digital glue that holds it all together."[9]

In fact, VerticalResponse reports businesses that use email marketing and engage in social media see a 28 percent higher email open rate, according to their user data. It's this combination that's powerful. "The numbers clearly show that those who broadcast content across multiple online touch points are getting a lot more engagement than those who don't," said VerticalResponse CEO Janine Popick.[10]

Rather than competing with one another for budget, these channels—email, social media, content marketing—actually complement one another quite nicely and can work in tandem to produce an effective, integrated marketing mix. Here are a few tips on how you can make your email marketing efforts more social—and vice versa.

In Your Email . . .

- Repackage and promote your content. If blogging is central to your content marketing, use your email as a promotional content roundup. Include paragraph-long snippets linking to full posts. While this may seem like overkill, you'd be surprised how many people miss your daily or weekly posts but find them in your emails. Again, the in-box is a special place for many and a key marketing opportunity for you. In addition to your blog posts, your latest videos, podcasts, and e-books can also gain additional promotional value in your emails.

- Say it with video. People like video. In fact, according to comScore, over 105 million Americans watch videos online each day.[11] As you can't play a video in an email (yet), make sure you are grabbing a screen-capture of your latest videos and including them in your emails. This visual cue is like clickable catnip for most readers who want to see what happens next.

— Tailor email content around social conversations. In your monthly newsletter (a popular type of email for many brands), drive readers to the content you post to your social channels. For example, if you posted photos from a recent event on Facebook, send your email traffic there as well.

— Put the spotlight on your followers. Speaking of getting something out of email and social media, most people love to be the center of attention. Why not take one of your most-active social media followers and interview them for your email newsletter? This also showcases an incentive to readers who might not be connected with you on social media yet.

— Include social media connect icons. In your email design (a big topic for another day or another book), find a way to integrate icons for the social platforms your brand is active on. Remember to include a strong call to action (why should they follow you?). These icons should link to your brand's social profiles. This is an important distinction to include, as you should also…

— Include social sharing icons. These icons allow readers to share your email content with their social networks, helping your ideas spread even further. Many applications such as

VerticalResponse and Constant Contact have tools for easily adding both types of buttons.

— Ask more bluntly to connect. While the icons should do the trick, they are also becoming so commonplace that your reader could tune them out. That's why it's a good idea to say it even more directly within your email content. If it's a newsletter, consider doing an article every now and then asking readers to connect on social media, explaining very clearly what they'll get out of it. If it's a letter-style email, try closing with a straightforward ask such as, "If you found this valuable, please consider taking a moment and connecting with us or sharing this with your social networks."

In Your Social Media and Content . . .

— Use social channels to mine for newsletter content. As you converse with your brand's communities on Facebook, Twitter, and other channels, find popular threads of discussion to explore via longer form content in your email newsletter. As noted previously, this newsletter content can also connect to your blog content.

— Post all hosted email links to your social networks. This is a rather elementary step but many marketers forget to do this. Email best practices tell us to have a link to a hosted version of our email content (usually a web page featuring the full email) at the top of the message in the preheader in case a subscriber's email client has images blocked. Be sure to share this link on your social channels as a reminder for fans to check their in-boxes. You might also expose your email content to social media fans who aren't signed up for your email program, which is why you also need to . . .

- Include email sign-up forms in social media. Remember, social media platforms may evolve but, by and large, email is forever. Ultimately you want your social media followers' email addresses in order to offer more personal forms of follow-up. Several email tools provide code or apps to create custom forms on Facebook pages, but you can also simply include links on your info and profile pages on other networks such as Twitter and LinkedIn. Don't forget your blog as an obvious social channel for capturing email addresses as well. If they want to make sure they receive all of your blog posts, they should subscribe to your email.

- Use email opt-in for gated content. While some of your content may be free and accessible, you may decide that some of your more proprietary content should be gated. Requiring email helps you drive leads and sales, while growing your email list.

One of my favorite examples of scrappy email and social media integration is so simple anyone can do it. And everyone should! The Iowa City Community School District might not be where you'd expect to find your organization's next big digital marketing idea. However, a 2013 email to their subscriber list provided a great tactic for driving social media engagement through email marketing. The email was simply a screenshot of their Facebook page with red circles around the like and share buttons with a subject line: Won't You Like Us?

The subject line alone invites enough curiosity to get you to open it (especially when your kid's school district is saying it). From there, they kept it pretty simple. Facebook's like button is a nice visual cue to drive action. While most people know where the like button is, many don't know where to go to share the page with their network, as this action is hidden in a drop-down menu. Expanding and circling this is both informative and actionable. Anyone can send out an email like this. Of course, the proof is in the pudding. A week after sending the email, the school district had nearly doubled the size of their Facebook audience.

By connecting your email clicks with your social media conversations and content, you can easily and effectively create a more integrated campaign, which will help you do more with less.

A POEM ON INTEGRATION

Sorry to get your hopes up but I don't have a poem for you. However, after email, it's easiest to discuss the other digital dots you need to connect through the POEM acronym. For those in need of a reminder, POEM encourages a mix of *p*aid, *o*wned, and *e*arned *m*edia. Poetic, isn't it?

Your paid advertising online comes in the form of pay-per-click and display ads on search engines and social networks. Owned media consists of your content (blogs, videos, podcasts) on a platform you own—your website, which you own or at least control the hosting of rather than platforms like Facebook and YouTube. Your earned media is . . . well, earned. This is the coverage you garner on other platforms you don't own. An example of this would be providing a guest post or infographic to another site in your industry as a means of driving awareness, traffic, and inbound links back to your brand.

All of these forms of media are critical to your brand's success. Let's take a look at how you can connect them.

GUESS WHAT? YOU STILL NEED TO PAY FOR ADS

After the happy dance marketers first do when they realize that many of our new forms of media are free, they quickly come back down to earth as they realize that there are indeed costs associated with all of these Shiny New Things in the form of personnel, graphic design, development, and more. It's a real cold bucket of water when they discover that they also haven't escaped paying for advertising exposure either.

The stalwart in this arena is Google's AdWords platform, which features both text-based pay-per-click (PPC) ads as well as visual display ads. These can be targeted around a variety of search options and geographic segments. As of 2015, this $50 billion business is a big part of what funds everything Google does. If this fact tells you nothing else, it should be pretty obvious that more than a few marketers are using Google AdWords.

Paid social media advertising is also becoming a growing part of marketers' plans. The Marketing Trends Survey from StrongView shows that the top areas of growth in social media budgets are paid marketing programs from Facebook and Twitter.[12] Paid advertising on Facebook, Twitter, and LinkedIn allows you to extend the reach of your brand's presence on these increasingly noisy channels by paying for additional exposure. Other platforms like Instagram, Snapchat, and Pinterest are also making the move into paid or sponsored exposure. Given the data these networks collect—especially rich profile insights on Facebook and LinkedIn—you can target who sees your brand with precision. You can also target special promotions and offers, driving traffic back to your website and, in turn, generating more leads and sales.

In maintaining our scrappy focus, we aren't going to switch gears and become a "PPC for Dummies" book. Instead, let's look at how you might connect your paid efforts with your organic social media and content marketing. If you look back at Part One of this book, you'll find another opportunity to ground your paid efforts in strategy. How can you align your paid programs around your larger digital marketing objectives?

Rather than building general awareness or promoting another offer, look for ways to connect your paid strategies with your social and content strategies to amplify your voice. If your lead generation efforts center around promoting problem-solving content, such as an e-book, consider adding a paid Facebook or LinkedIn campaign targeting those in geographic areas that match your customer profile and work in the industry you are targeting.

Monetate, a provider of cloud-based technology for online marketers, looked at their website referrals and saw an opportunity to bolster the traffic that their social presences on Facebook, Twitter, and LinkedIn were driving. Through a mix of Facebook and Linked In ads and promoted tweets (Twitter's paid ads that amplify specific tweets), Monetate saw a 15 percent increase in website referrals from social media.

"Unfortunately, when it comes to reaching your fans and followers, owned media is no guarantee," says Rob Yoegel, Monetate's former content marketing director, who now leads marketing at Gaggle. "To better understand where your most valuable customers and prospects are, look at your inbound referral traffic and devote some of your paid media approach to the top channels. For instance, for social media, consider the LIFT approach. LIFT stands for LinkedIn, Facebook, and Twitter, but will also result in a lift in traffic, leads, and sales. Keep in mind that for your business, one social channel may provide more value than another, but by devoting even a small portion of a paid media budget to LIFT, you will see the impact these channels can have on your business."[13]

Again, there are too many great resources to count when it comes to paid search and social media advertising. Instead of focusing on what you're doing specifically, the scrappy approach focuses on how you get this done and, more importantly, how you can connect your paid online advertising back to your bigger digital marketing map.

- - - - - - - - - - - - - -

OWNED MEDIA, ORGANIC SEARCH, AND OPTIMIZATION

When it comes to connecting the dots of your owned media—specifically your content—your primary focus becomes optimizing what you're creating with what people are already searching for. This is that SEO or search-engine optimization thing you've probably heard something about. Marcus Sheridan (Chapter 4) didn't intuitively reinvent River Pools' blog. He analyzed search data from Google's Keyword Tool (now known as the Google Keyword Planner) to learn more about what kind of content he could create that would provide value to his customers and potential customers. Using search data on the front end of his content development efforts helped him create a site that quickly became a trusted resource within the industry at large.

This is another one of those small process points that's easy to miss, but that can pay off in the long run. Instead of racking your brain over what topics you should cover, examine what people are already searching for and start from there. These insights could also prove useful in populating your conversation calendar for social media. If people are searching for these topics, they might be looking for conversations to participate in on Twitter and LinkedIn as well.

Beyond considering search as a means of planning your work, you can also optimize your finished content for search using blogging tools like WordPress SEO from Yoast. This simple plug-in gamifies the painstaking task of ensuring that your post has keywords in all of the right places for the search terms you want your content associated with.

Other forms of content such as videos can be optimized as well. It doesn't hurt that YouTube, the most popular video player, is owned by Google, the most popular search engine. Furthermore, YouTube itself is the second most popular search engine. It's easy to breeze through all of the fields when uploading your YouTube videos, but taking the time to align your title and tags with the keywords you want to focus on can help ensure that your content shows up in searches on both of these online giants.

As much as keywords and consistency have come up, try creating a list of your organization's top 10 keywords and keyword combinations that you want to focus on. By sharing this keyword bank internally, you can make sure everyone is on the same page; unifying their work with yours can help your marketing dollars go further. Remember the lesson from Chapter 5. Your team members can't help you if they don't know what it is you're trying to do. This is especially true at larger organizations where one team is creating content and social media conversations while another is optimizing the company's website.

Better internal communication is critical in maximizing the effectiveness and efficiency of your marketing.

EARNED MEDIA FOR THE WIN

In thinking about the various pieces of the POEM acronym, you can quickly see that all of these bases are important to cover when building a robust digital marketing plan. Without an owned platform at the center, you are potentially building a house on rented property. The benefits of all of the traffic you drive to your site accumulate over time. Because these organic benefits take a lot of time and effort to realize, you need to reinforce this work through paid campaigns. Cost-effective search and social ads are great at expanding your reach beyond your customers and those who have already connected with you.

Outside of the paid and organic traffic you drive to your site, the final component or digital dot you need to connect is earned media. By its very definition, earned media cannot be bought. It can only be gained organically, or *earned*. Traditionally, earned media was the publicity that resulted from either our paid advertising or public relations campaigns. Digital technologies have expanded the power of earned media and has potentially turned everyone—even individuals—into influential media platforms.

What does this mean for your earned media online? Beyond your PR team's work pitching your organization to media outlets, they are likely identifying influential bloggers and social media personalities. By appealing to like-minded individuals or organizations, you gain opportunities for guest blogs, news coverage, product reviews, or webinars. In many respects, you become an external content provider for their platform. In the end, your brand gets both increased visibility and authority.

As earned media is as much an art as a science, your integration will more than likely take place at the strategic level, making yet another case for sharing your map internally. If you're working on building your brand, you might work with your PR team (which could be you, as well) on an earned campaign connected to your larger digital strategy by identifying influential bloggers and providing them with valuable content for their audience.

Beyond offering additional brand exposure and inbound links, your earned media partnerships can help other areas of your digital strategy as well. For example, if you provide a webinar for an important industry blog, you might seek permission to repurpose this content on your own platform after a set amount of time. We'll discuss repurposing your content in greater depth in the next chapter.

As one of the most trusted forms of marketing available—consider the value of word-of-mouth referrals amplified online—earned media should be an integral part of your digital marketing strategy.

THE SUM OF OUR TOUCH POINTS

As new forms of media emerge at an increasingly rapid pace, it's easy to create unnecessary organizational silos. We assume that our digital team has to move faster than everyone else so we end up siloing them off from the rest of marketing. As email and websites have been around for a while, those teams may not move as fast as our emerging social platforms. As a result, in larger organizations, we even silo our various forms of digital marketing. At the end of the day, however, it's all marketing.

"Don't think of digital as a channel," cautions Daniel Rowles, author of *Digital Branding.* "It's the sum of all of your touch points."[14] We have to get past our internal silos. Our customers don't see these differences between the channels where they interact with us. They're looking for a unified brand experience, an idea we'll expand upon in Chapter 9. However, to create a foundation for that experience we have to first connect our digital dots.

Like the smart steps presented in Part One of this book, connecting these dots helps us put our brains before our budget. Better integration among our digital marketing touch points like social media and email marketing also continues the theme we've been building upon in Part Two, where we've focused on how to do more with less. Questions have the power to fuel your content and spark social media conversations. You have to seek them out and bank them for future use. Your team can help you do this if you embrace your people power and get them off of the bench and into the game. All of this helps create more effective and efficient marketing, like the mousetrap of the scrappy mindset.

With a smart plan in place and a framework for how we can do more with less, it's time to look ahead. How can you simplify your marketing even further for the long haul?

 **NEXT STEPS**

Here's where you begin connecting your digital dots.

— Start a list of your online touch points now and see where you can connect them.

— Why should someone bother to follow your brand on social media? Remember to spell out these benefits clearly when it comes time to add the social media icons to your other brand touch points—both online and off.

— How can you integrate your email marketing with your social media and content marketing? Remember, email is the digital glue that holds your customer relationships together.

— How can you use your paid search and social media advertising to amplify your current marketing efforts?

— Check out Google's Keyword Planner (https://adwords .google.com/KeywordPlanner) and review the top keyword combinations in your industry. How can you create owned media content around the heavily searched keywords and combinations you uncover?

— Who are the online influencers in your industry? If you're having trouble answering this, consider who your customers listen to. How can you identify them and find ways to partner on new forms of content, which can help you drive more earned media traffic back to your brand?

Part Three

SIMPLIFY FOR THE LONG HAUL

Chapter 7

THE SIMPLIFICATION GAME

Siegel+Gale is one of the world's leading strategic branding and design firms. Founded in 1969 by Alan Siegel, the company helps a wide range of global clients build clear, credible, compelling brands that drive their businesses forward. Armed with the philosophy that "simple is smart," Siegel+Gale develops brand strategies, stories, and experiences that inspire employees, motivate customers, and make their clients stand out in an increasingly complex world.

When I interviewed David B. Srere, Siegel+Gale's co-CEO and chief strategy officer, about the value of simplicity, he explained that "When communications and processes are simplified to their core, they're easier to understand, they break through the clutter, and they resonate more deeply with people." But Srere cautioned that achieving simplicity isn't easy, joking that "As the old saying goes, 'if I had more time, I would have written a shorter letter. '"[1]

While we may not own up to it, one of the concepts that most of us believe in is that more is better. More time spent on a plan makes it better. More meetings means something is more thought out. More money exchanged promises a widget that will do the job better. The truth is, more isn't always better. Sometimes (often?) more is just more.

One of the places that's hard to recognize this truth is with digital marketing. You can't click on a marketing best practices article without seeing that people are consuming more content as they continue to spend more time on social media. Heeding this battle cry, marketers have drastically upped their content and social media marketing. We're churning out more content and social media conversations than ever before. When we fall prey to rote Checklist Marketing, we end up less effective and efficient over time.

To make your marketing even better, you have to simplify these pain points. That is, you must *simplify* the complexities that arise as you adopt and implement social media and content marketing for the long haul. These new forms of digital marketing require a significant investment of time that many marketers aren't prepared for. With a smart plan in place and a system for doing more with less, you have to look ahead and simplify your marketing even more to help you out over time.

As best-selling author and strategist Jay Baer said of the relationship between content marketing and social media, "Content is fire, social media is the gasoline."[2] We can't get social and start conversations without helpful content to share with our community. To get started, here are some strategies for simplifying content marketing.

- - - - - - - - - - - - - - - - - - -
THE TOP PROBLEMS COMPLICATING CONTENT (AND WHAT TO DO ABOUT THEM)

As noted earlier, data from the Content Marketing Institute (CMI) and MarketingProfs show that content marketing is being used by at least 90 percent of all organizations across all sectors—B2C, B2B, and nonprofit.[3] Nearly half of these marketers are looking to spend more on content marketing in the years ahead.[4] However, work in this area can get complicated. Let's take a look at some of the most challenging obstacles and how you can overcome them.

No Content Strategy— Among the other key findings in the CMI/MarketingProfs data is the fact that over 50 percent of marketers lack a documented content strategy.[5] As I've stressed since Part One of this book, anything worth doing is worth doing right. And the only way to know what's right is to ground your content marketing with a smart plan. You have to answer three big questions: *Why are you doing this? What are you trying to do? Who are you trying to reach?* A lack of strategy leads you to creating content inefficiently, which further complicates your marketing.

Not Enough Content— If you read the data from CMI/Marketing-Profs[6] and Google's Zero Moment of Truth,[7] you'll see that marketers are struggling to create enough content in an online marketplace where consumers are looking for twice as much content to help them make purchase decisions. Marketers today can't keep up. Part of the problem is that most marketers have . . .

No Consistent Content Schedule— While it's sort of true that the Internet has made everyone a publisher, it's a shame we haven't learned more from the publishing industry. One practice that many brands need to borrow from traditional publishers is setting a consistent schedule and editorial calendar. (Remember, in Chapter 4 I noted that a simple calendar should be your new best friend.) In addition to establishing audience expectations, this also helps you develop your own content creation muscles and routine. However this gets tricky when you have . . .

No Time to Create Content— *We need more content! We need to produce it more regularly!* But when does all of this get done? Many marketers are burdened with the time it takes to produce even a minimal amount of content. *There's got to be a better way!* There is and it lies in getting your fellow employees involved in your content creation efforts. Content marketing is a huge outlay in time, talent, and treasure. You have to look for efficiencies. You have to embrace your people power.

Not Enough Different Forms of Content— Too often marketers forget that different consumers require different forms of content. Don't get lured into a homogeneous approach to your content. Take the time to consider your various audience segments and their unique needs at all stages of your buying cycle. This will help you create diverse content in both short and long forms.

As you can see, all of these factors can potentially complicate your content marketing. How do you clear these complex hurdles? Following the smart steps from Part One can establish a sound content marketing strategy. Once approved, you need to employ the frameworks for doing more with less we looked at in Part Two. How can you fuel your content with questions? How can you get your people involved in your content creation? How can you connect your content with the rest of your digital channels for more effective and efficient marketing?

While this lens can simplify these content complexities, I'd like to share four additional hacks that can help you do even more with less when it comes to your content marketing.

FOUR CONTENT CREATION HACKS THAT
BELONG IN EVERY MARKETER'S TOOLBOX

Content creation can get real complex real fast. That's why there are four content creation hacks that should be in every marketer's toolbox. These tips and tricks epitomize the scrappy mindset and help us bring it to life in our marketing.

Hack #1: Relentlessly Repurposing Content— In *Content Rules*, Ann Handley and C.C. Chapman invite brands to be "content chopshops" by always looking to get more than one use out of a particular piece of content.[8] You can take this a step further and relentlessly repurpose your content. So how does one go about doing this? Let's start small.

For many, creating longer-form content such as e-books or white papers can be daunting. A little mindful repurposing can provide you with a plan and a scrappy way to build internal confidence among your team. Start by planning your e-book or white paper's table of contents. Based on this outline, write each chapter or section as an individual blog post. With this content mapped out on your editorial calendar, you'll have an e-book in no time and lots of blog content along the way. Not to mention invaluable feedback that can only enhance each chapter.

That said, there's no reason you couldn't put this strategy in reverse and take a larger piece of content apart to use as individual blog posts. Your goal should be to create content (write something, shoot video, etc.) *once* and find multiple formats in which to publish that same content. Here are a few additional ideas on how you can relentlessly repurpose your content.

- (1) Blog posts could be threaded together as a (2) presentation, which could then have (3) slides that are uploaded to SlideShare and (4) embedded in yet another blog post recapping your presentation.

- (1) A series of Instagram photos could be combined to form (2) a Facebook album, which could then be the basis for (3) a slide show video with a voiceover, which could then be (4) embedded on another blog post.

- (1) An About video for your business could be (2) embedded on a web page or blog post transcribing the video and making it (3) SEO-friendly content on your site.

For example, Pew Research relentlessly repurposes by (1) sharing individual data points on Instagram, (2) which point to a longer blog post about the research, (3) which then invites you to download the entire study.

Relentlessly repurposing your content also provides another opportunity for you to get your team involved. Make reimagining your content an internal challenge by encouraging others to offer ideas on additional forms of content you could get out of a recent blog post or e-book. A fresh set of eyes will often see new opportunities the content creator might have missed. Over time, it becomes a fun game to play and an effective way to do more with less.

Hack #2: Utilizing Historical Content— Another form of content you may not think to reimagine is your company's historical content. If your business has any kind of history, chances are there are files and boxes of old photos in some storage closet or facility. One of the scrappiest things you can do is have an intern digitize this old-school content so that you can give it new life online.

Whether it's #ThrowbackThursday on Instagram or populating Facebook's timeline milestones on your brand page, these content classics are a tremendous asset if you have them. Office furniture giant Herman Miller has a Pinterest board called "107 Years and Counting" featuring photos of their founders, old products, and more. Even your old marketing collateral and advertisements offer some nice history. Southwest Airlines has a Pinterest board dedicated entirely to their old ads.

Hack #3: Curating Content— Beyond finding ways to repurpose as much of your brand's internal content as possible, there are other sources you can lean on outside your organization. As there's so much great content being created today, content curation—selecting the best content to share with your community—can be a valuable skill. It's also another way you can feed your consumers' hungry appetite for more content.

You can share curated content several ways. For example, you can create a blog post or email newsletter that rounds up the best articles in your industry or on a particular subject in a simple hyperlinked list (remember to offer proper attribution and link back to the original content). With budgets stretched thin and an audience with expanding content needs, curation is a viable part of the mix for many organizations, especially those in industries that are already saturated with content. Over time, your brand can become valuable to your audience as the official "wine taster" in your industry due to your discerning palate.

There are several tools that can help you streamline the task of finding good content. Some are free or low-cost—like Feedly,

Scoop.it, Newsle—and some are geared more toward the mid-market or enterprise level with more functionality and features, such as Curata and TrapIt. One note of caution: Avoid thinking of curation as simply a low-cost alternative to content creation. While they are certainly lower, there are costs associated with content curation (technology platform, employee time, etc.). More importantly, you still need to build up your own content. Curation and creation should be viewed as complementary approaches to the same overall strategy—providing your community with useful content.

Hack #4: Encouraging User-Generated Content— The final external hack is empowering your community to be a part of your marketing. User-generated content is valuable in more ways than one. First, to be very frank, it's content you don't have to create that you can turn around and share again, which brings us to the second benefit. User-generated content is powerful as it demonstrates in a very public way that your audience likes you and is engaged.

A common misconception is that user-generated content just appears. Like all things involving others, it starts with a request from you. Remember, no one, your customers and community included, will know what to do unless you ask them. As you do this, work to start a larger conversation beyond "upload your photo!" If your brand is connected to a specific business, industry, or a need or cause, look for ways to tie your user-generated content campaign to something bigger. When this content is shared it creates conversations and a greater sense of community between you, the brand, and your audience.

After Ben & Jerry's discovered tons of photos featuring their fans sharing their love for their product, they turned it into a campaign by asking fans to share their best ecstatic photos using the hashtag #CaptureEuphoria. The favorites were then featured in ads for the brand. The campaign's community involvement is in the larger story about over-the-top experiences—not just ice cream.[9]

All four of these approaches—relentlessly repurposing content, utilizing historical content, content curation, and user-generated content—provide useful hacks as you work to simplify your content both internally and externally.

WHEN IT COMES TO GOOD CONTENT, LESS IS MORE

Strategist, speaker, and author Mark W. Schaefer points out another problem with this prolific level of content production we find ourselves in. At some point very soon, with marketers creating more and more content, we will exceed the number of eyeballs in existence to actually consume all of this content.[10] What's a marketer to do? Keep creating more content and hope that people find it?

In looking at the research from the Content Marketing Institute and MarketingProfs, we see that marketers struggle with creating content that engages.[11] Beyond the blood, sweat, and tears it takes to make even a basic blog post or video, it turns out that quality is a huge factor impeding our content marketing success. Engaging content is also critical to standing out from the crowd.

This is especially true when you consider that many marketers are churning out "me-too" content without thinking. Without coming up with a unique frame or worldview to apply. Without being able to answer the question "Why should this content exist?" much less "Why should anyone read it?" When I interviewed Purematter CEO Bryan Kramer, author of *Shareology* and *H2H*, he urged marketers to "Pick one or two things instead of trying to do everything."[12] It's not about producing more content. It's about producing *better* content. Even if you're creating less content as a result.

Though producing enough content is keeping marketers up at night, it's nothing compared to the challenge of producing better content. Anyone can write a "me-too" blog post or create a video "like the one that went viral." However, the results are a distant echo of the original at best. Creating better content requires a strategy on what to say and a unique brand voice to bring it to life. Producing enough content is just the tip of the iceberg.

Remember, when it comes to your content marketing, more isn't always better. Sometimes more is just more. Grounded with strategy and a few helpful hacks to simplify your content, let's move on to simplifying your social media conversations.

A COMPLICATED SOCIAL SITUATION

Social media seems so simple at the outset. *A platform where we update our customers and community on what we're up to? Easy!* If only. Once again, we usually end up complicating things, often under the guise of making them better. In simplifying content creation, we uncovered a problem that was at the root of many of our most common content challenges. That root problem is the fact that most marketers are flying blind without a strategy, which unnecessarily complicates content creation. There's a similar root problem when it comes to keeping our social media conversations simple as well.

Social media is . . . well, social. It's gained the attention it has by being fundamentally different from all of the media channels that preceded it. All of a sudden, the audience can (and does) talk back. We can have real conversations with our audience now. These conversations help us build close relationships with our customers. In some complex, layered industries, these direct relationships weren't even possible before. However, with this added degree of connectivity, we have to be ready for negative customer interactions.

This can be scary. In some cases, this fear keeps brands from engaging on social media altogether. Concerns over negative social media interactions with our customers can complicate our time spent focusing on these new channels. Many marketers are consumed by the following issues stemming from what could go wrong with social media.

- *What if someone says something bad about us?*

- *How do we handle negative comments?*

- *How soon should we respond?*

We spend excessive amounts of time overthinking these negative what-ifs and not nearly enough time focusing on what really matters, building those close relationships. How can we better engage our most passionate followers? To fully exorcise the items that we shouldn't be wasting our time on, let's lay these compacting factors to rest by simplifying them.

Issue #1: Receiving Negative Comments— As the old adage goes, your unhappy customers tell 10 people while your happy customers may not tell anyone at all. With help from social media, your angry customers can now tell 10 friends and their friends' friends and so on. But what's the real motivation behind sharing these grievances? According to *The Social Habit* from Edison Research, 79 percent of those complaining about a brand on Twitter did so in hopes that their "friends would see it." While 52 percent hoped "the company would see it," only 36 percent expected that the brand would "see it and address the problem."[13]

Solution: Overcome customers' low expectations of brand

responsiveness online by looking for ways that you can surprise them and overdeliver. While complaining customers may not be looking for you to respond when they're upset, you'll find yourself with an incredible opportunity—albeit a scary one initially—if you take a deep breath and engage. Have a simple plan in place with your service or support team for dealing with upset customers and put it to work each time there's a problem.

Issue #2: Deleting Negative Comments— After you solve the problem you delete the negative comment, right? Wrong. In *Likeable Social Media*, strategist Dave Kerpen encourages brands to follow a Do-Not-Delete Rule, stating that "unless a comment is obscene, profane, bigoted, or contains someone's personal or private information, never delete it from a social network."[14] Leaving a trail of your successful issue resolution online is just as important as addressing the initial customer problem. Doing so not only shows that you're listening and responding, it also shows that you're a transparent organization with real people behind it. Humans make mistakes and, more often than not, consumers understand and forgive when we own up to our slip-ups.

Solution: If there are aspects of your brand experience that aren't always sunny, don't hide from them. In fact, there may be more to gain from addressing these challenges head on through your content. Palmer College of Chiropractic encourages student bloggers to talk about the good and the bad days in their posts. This gives prospective students insight on what life is going to be like when they go through this intensive program. This kind of approach also helps demonstrate your brand's transparency.

"We believe the more we can share with our audience, the more they trust that we care about them and their education," adds Katie Merritt, communications coordinator at Palmer.[15] Learning to accept and integrate negative conversations and content is just one of the many shifts that social media has brought about. In the end, benefits like earning trust outweigh those uneasy feelings we get in our stomach when the negative notifications first appear.

Issue #3: Response Time—While it's easy for your inner social media purist to pipe up and say you should always respond "immediately or it doesn't count and you're doing it wrong"—the real answer on how soon you should engage is much more complicated and dependent on many internal and external factors. First of all, to sound like a broken record, your optimal response time is largely dictated by what your brand is doing on social media in the first place. If you can't answer this in a few words, it might be symptomatic of a larger issue (and probably a good sign you should go back to Part One of the book). For example, if your strategy is built around using Twitter for customer service, this might merit a more immediate response than managing a brand-driven community on Facebook or Pinterest.

Solution: You need to find a social media plan and pace that works for you. Once you've done this, a helpful but oft-missed step is communicating this plan to your community. Some brands even go so far as noting the hours a Facebook page or Twitter account is staffed front and center on the page or account descriptions. Pancheros, whose scrappy two-person social staffing we discussed in Chapter 5, makes a point of not scheduling social posts at times when they can't respond as readily.[16] If you're actively listening to your community you may start to observe that your fans and followers are more or less hungry for responses than you initially thought. If they're requiring more care and feeding than your current internal resources allow, you may need to invest in more people, better tools, or external agency support.

From here, we're free to focus on what's more important—using social media to build close relationships with your customers.

— — — — — — — — — — — — —
FOCUSING ON THE RIGHT
PEOPLE: A SIMPLE SOLUTION

The best strategy for simplifying your social media conversations is to focus your attention on the right people. As you probably know from your own experience as well as the three issues we just discussed, we tend to focus a substantial amount of time on what happens when/if things go wrong. We also focus a disproportionate amount of attention on the followers we don't have yet in our quest to build the biggest social following. *We need more likes on our Facebook page! We need more followers on Twitter! More! More! MORE!* Okay, but then what? And, more importantly, what about the most important group that we totally lose sight of?

Our most important customer group online is also our most underserved—our brand advocates. Beyond worrying about how to grow social followings and what happens when someone gets mad, few marketers take the time to focus on their most passionate customers who are already following them and engaging with their brand. Just as you develop plans for audience growth and crisis management, you should also create a system for elevating your very best, most ardent customers and rewarding them. It's a shame that so few are doing this. When brands do take this extra step of reaching out to their most committed followers, they reap rewards and usually end up increasing their audience exposure in the long run.

Why are so many ignoring this group? The answer itself is simple. It's easy to forget about this group unless you have a discovery process in place for listening and escalating mentions from your raving fans. While there are certainly enterprise-level solutions like

Salesforce Marketing Cloud, you can also find less expensive tools such as Sprout Social and HootSuite. Regardless of your listening system, before you can treat this group any differently, you need a concrete process in place. Let's look at a couple of brands reaching out and elevating their passionate followers.

Each Wednesday at 10:00 A.M. Central, a Twitter chat aptly called #BrandChat focuses on the topic of branding. When I can, I try to drop in to listen and learn. One week I joined the conversation after a morning run and mentioned being hungry for a Chobani Greek yogurt. Moments later Chobani popped into the conversation offering to send a treat to anyone on the chat who emailed them. Following a friendly exchange about what yogurt flavors are most popular at our house (because who wouldn't respond to a tweet in exchange for free yogurt?), they sent me a care package. This helped escalate me from a basic follower to a fan in Chobani's eyes. This relationship was furthered during the 2012 Summer Olympics when they sent me a gift pack of Chobani-branded Olympic swag, transforming me from fan to brand advocate.

And the story doesn't end there. They've now included me in a special group that gets occasional new yogurt flavors for testing. How cool is that? First, in terms of customer loyalty and retention, it's a good example of escalating customer commitment. Second, it allows Chobani to get market research and feedback from a high-volume customer at a minimal cost.

In planning your brand's outreach you need to think of all of these actions as steps in a fan escalation system. Chobani first reached out unexpectedly, demonstrating superb listening skills and elevated select customers to their inner circle with a free gift that, though it was not free for them, cost very little in the grand scheme of things. Next, they continued reaching out to their inner circle during their Olympic sponsorship, which had a large social focus.

Finally, they rewarded long-term advocacy by providing exclusive product access.

Tamsen Webster of Oratium (we met her in Chapter 5) often speaks on maximizing influencer outreach. She has identified four types of social influencers on the axes of connections (broad vs. personal) and probability of action: Connected Catalysts, Passionate Publishers, Everyday Advocates, and Altruistic Activators (see Figure 7.1).

Figure 7.1: The Four Types of Social Influencers
(*Source:* Tamsen Webster)

When it comes to outreach, many marketers think only of those with broad-reaching connections (highly connected social influencers like tech maven Robert Scoble), while missing the fact that your Altruistic Activators can often deliver just as much action on behalf of your brand. Though this group often has a fraction of the following of the Connected Catalysts, your outreach is more likely to deliver an impactful "*Wow!*" to that individual user, prompting more advocacy than you might get from superusers—if you're lucky enough to land on their radar.

The example Webster often cites is her experience with eyeglasses game-changer Warby Parker (a favorite company of your bespectacled author). Tamsen has documented many cases, including her own, where passionate fans felt the need to rise up and answer their friends' questions on where to get glasses. In many instances, fans' mentions of Warby Parker on Twitter are serving as the brand's listening system, after which Warby Parker often jumps in with recommendations and assistance, as Chobani did with me.

Warby Parker ensures such strong fan coverage via outreach to all influencers on the grid—from highly Connected Catalysts like Ashton Kutcher to those like Tamsen, who have significantly smaller followings when compared to Kutcher, but with great commitment to the brand within their own networks. Warby Parker rewards this advocacy by treating passionate fans to moments of "*Wow!*" such as the video Webster received from Santa Claus at the Warby store in New York City, wishing her a Merry Christmas by name.

Developing a system for elevating and rewarding your most passionate fans might sound more complex than simple. However, the simplicity comes from shifting your focus to your best brand advocates. Rather than exhausting resources on gaining more followers for the sake of having more followers and *over*planning what to do if you have an upset customer, you'll find yourself doing more with less if you focus instead on those most committed to your brand.

THE MOST IMPORTANT STEP TO SIMPLIFYING YOUR SOCIAL MEDIA MARKETING

Sorry. This final step isn't a simple hack, tool, or platform. Instead, it's a reminder of something I first mentioned back in Chapter 2. That's the perception gap, which told us that while 76 percent of marketers feel they know what their customers want, only 34 percent have bothered to ask.[17] Don't make this mistake. Remember the old saying, "to assume makes an ass of you and me." Let's remember not to be assuming asses when it comes to our social media conversations. This is a channel defined by your ability to listen, not just talk.

All of this starts by first asking your community what they're looking for from your brand. After asking this—*stop!* And listen. Once you've gathered real insights on what you can do to provide meaningful conversations, more of your work is done than you realize. Just as strategy was the rudder guiding our content simplification, we can similarly steer our social conversations by listening. Like the relationships we build offline, it's easy to forget to listen. Talking is easier and requires less thinking. Too often we take the same approach online. But listening can be the very foundation of building close relationships. Don't squander this opportunity.

Remember, more isn't always better. Sometimes more is just more. To simplify your marketing, you need to focus on the conversations and content that deliver the highest yield in terms of audience engagement. To get at this, you have to measure what matters. This too is easier said than done.

 **NEXT STEPS**

Now it's your turn to start simplifying your content and social media marketing.

— Before you start creating content, revisit the smart steps from Part One to create a scrappy content strategy. *Why are you doing this? Who are you creating this for?* Answering those questions will help you get a better grasp on what you should be doing.

- Remember the four content creation hacks:

  - *Relentlessly repurpose content:* The next time you create a piece of content, brainstorm how many other things you can create from it.

  - *Utilize historic content:* Dig into your files. Go into that old storage unit. Are there old photos you can digitize into relevant throwback content?

  - *Curate content:* Where is great content already being created that you can share with your online community? Can you make this a regular part of your content strategy?

  - *Encourage user-generated content:* Ask for it! Your customers will only know what you need if you ask them.

- Take a step back. Are you creating too much content? Or perhaps too much "me-too" content? How can you create something better, even if it means creating less content over time?

- What's your plan for dealing with upset customers and negative comments on social media? Create a plan and implement it. Stop dwelling on the negative.

- Instead, consider how can you transform your happy customers online into loyal social brand ambassadors? Just as you develop a system for dealing with upset customers, you need a plan in place for elevating your happy customers.

- All of this starts with better online listening. What's your plan for accomplishing this critical task?

Chapter 8

MEASURE WHAT MATTERS

Marketers famously have a love/hate relationship with measurement. We know all of the great quotes, from Peter Drucker's "You can't manage what you don't measure" to Tom Peters' "What gets measured gets done." We've used them in PowerPoint decks. We have them up on our office walls. We get it. Measurement is important. And, as marketers, we should be proud of our work and eager to point to our successes.

For small businesses, measurement is essential, as we can't afford to waste precious marketing resources, such as time and money, on things that don't perform. For big businesses, though being efficient is still key, the ability to demonstrate the success of our marketing ensures that we'll have more of those resources down the road.

So why the reluctance to roll up our sleeves and dig in when it comes to measurement? If strategy is like the vegetables we don't want to eat, then measurement is like that root canal we don't want to undergo—but it sure beats the alternative. Historically, measurement has been an area of contention between the right and left brainers, with the creative marketers pushing back on measuring their mysterious arts and the business analysts (I originally had "bean counters" there if that tips my hand) trying to apply comprehensive accountability to every penny spent. Consequently, digital marketing measurement is weighed down with a lot of baggage.

In this penultimate chapter, with the rest of our marketing planned and executed, let's take a look at how we can measure what matters, simplify our metrics, and share our successes. Let's start with some of that measurement baggage.

A BRIEF HISTORY OF MARKETING MEASUREMENT

Remember that historic marketing timeline we reviewed in Chapter 1? If you recall, in the beginning, there were print advertisements. These created general awareness and helped the businesses that used them sell more of their wares. The blacksmith sold more horseshoes. The general store couldn't keep enough rock candy in stock. Everyone was happy.

Through the years, we started focusing on how we could be a bit more precise with our marketing. In the late 19th century, Montgomery Ward began sending out catalogs you could order from directly and a new industry was born, though it wasn't called direct marketing until 1967 when Lester Wunderman, father of the 1-800 number, coined the phrase. Marketers enthusiastically embraced this approach because they could simplify their efforts by focusing on the promotions and products that had the highest yield and delivered results.

If that was all there was to the history of marketing measurement, we wouldn't have as much baggage, as the descendants and core values of direct-response marketing and advertising are still alive and well in the form of email marketing, paid search and social media advertising, and other digital channels. Things got tricky in the 20th century with the birth and widespread popularity of mass media through radio and television. Radio ads grabbed the attention of listeners in ways that print ads never could. The jingles were catchy and fun! Television delivered marketing messages to families right in their own living rooms. The talking box could show pretty pictures of your product or business that looked awesome! *Let's get some of those!* TV commercials appeal to all of the senses! And marketers were happy again. Kind of.

You see, broadcast media also carried a bigger price tag. But it looked and sounded cool and gave you an entire new battery of tools you could employ creatively to stand out in an increasingly noisy marketplace. However, it wasn't just the price that was a tough pill to swallow. It was the fact that these forms of media were challenging to measure. *How many people saw or heard my ad? And how many of them came into my store as a result? And how many of them actually bought something?* Marketers came to rely on sample-based systems like the Nielsen (television) and Arbitron (radio) ratings that could give a general snapshot of the audience size and composition, but offered little to no ad-performance data.

As a result, massive industries emerged built around TV and radio advertising (the more ads you buy, the more shelf space you can acquire to sell more products, which provides more income to buy more ads, and so on). To resolve the cognitive dissonance on whether or not this model actually worked, we started lying to ourselves about measurement, making it a little more imperfect. Traditional media was imperfect, so everything else needed to be as well. We laughed off the famous quip from merchant turned marketing pioneer John Wanamaker, who said, "Half the money I spend on advertising is wasted; the trouble is I don't know which half."

Unmeasured media ruined measurement for the rest of marketing, as most of us now wring our hands over the task of measuring our work. Some of this is brought on by the fact that, as marketers, we're under more scrutiny than ever to justify our performance. An annual survey from the Association of National Advertisers shows that accountability or "developing and measuring return on marketing investments . . . what to measure, and how to move from measurement to action" remains a chief concern among marketers.[1]

The good news is that, just as it's an exciting time to be in marketing, it's an equally exciting time to be measuring it.

A GOOD PROBLEM TO HAVE

Make no mistake about it, our new digital marketing channels have no shortage of numbers. It's actually the exact opposite of traditional broadcast media. While there are a ton of numbers now, there's also a catch. As sociologist William Bruce Cameron once said, "Everything that can be counted does not necessarily count. Everything that counts cannot necessarily be counted." This quote perfectly sums up the biggest challenge marketers face when it comes to measuring their digital efforts.

We have an abundance of numbers when it comes to social media and content marketing. Data from Altimeter Group shows us that that most marketers are using a mix of engagement data (likes, followers), sentiment (positive vs. negative), and website traffic as the top sources of measurement.[2] To dig a little deeper on this, engagement data is composed of various forms of data that are, in many cases, readily available to the general public. A look at a brand's Facebook page or Twitter account can yield basic engagement data. On the content side of things, engagement data could include the number of comments on a blog post or views on a YouTube video.

Engagement data includes:

- Likes

- Followers

- Mentions

- Retweets

- Shares

- Subscribers

- Comments

- Favorites

- Clicks

Sentiment offers a little more insight as this data point, usually found using paid tools from platforms such as Salesforce Marketing Cloud, tells you whether these online conversations are good or bad in nature. For example, by measuring engagement data alone, an airline might find that their tweets, retweets, and mentions are up. However, when viewed through the lens of sentiment, they may see that 90 percent of this activity was negative. Two different metrics—engagement data and sentiment—tell two very different stories.

The next most common source of data is *website analytics*. The most widely used tool for measuring website analytics is Google Analytics, which is used by nearly half of the 1,000,000 most popular websites as tracked by Alexa.[3] Google Analytics has free and premium versions of their service, which use tracking codes embedded on your website or blog to provide robust reporting on traffic sources, audience demographics and behaviors, and much more.

Website analytics include:

- **Visitors:** new vs. old

- **Session:** time on site

- **Traffic sources:** direct, referring sites, search

- **Adwords:** paid advertising integration

- **Goal conversions:** following particular marketing paths you set as goals

- **Platform or device:** type of device audience uses

- **Geographic network:** where your audience is located

- **Page tracking:** path followed through your site

- **Internal search:** what they're looking for on your site

- **Site speed:** website performance

- **Social interactions:** how they engage on your site

- **Audience:** age/gender

A problem with both engagement data and website analytics is that, while they certainly tell a story, it's a basic story at best and not necessarily one that's connected to your business objective or the destination at the end of your marketing map. As Jason Falls, senior vice president of digital strategy at Elasticity and author of *No Bullshit Social Media*, has said, "You can't make payroll with likes or comments. You can't pay your mortgage with page views or clickthroughs. Engagement only takes you so far. You have to create conversion from that engagement or you're not accomplishing anything truly meaningful to a business."[4]

The first step in simplifying your metrics so you can measure what matters is aligning your measurement with the rest of your marketing strategy.

COOKING UP MEANINGFUL METRIC RECIPES

When I teach digital marketing at the University of Iowa, I often have students read about measurement first, as a lead-in to discussing how to plan a marketing strategy. As scrappy marketers, we need to be thinking about the end (measurement) back at the beginning (planning strategy) as well.

If we go back to Chapters 2 and 3, we spent a lot of time focusing on defining your destination—*what business objective are you working toward accomplishing?* As a reminder, the most common marketing destinations are:

- Branding

- Community building

- Public relations

- Market research

- Customer service

- Lead generation/sales

If you've selected one or two of these that you are trying to accomplish, then you know what you're working toward. To measure this, you need to align the many numbers you have at your command around these core objectives. The good news is, as evidenced from the data reviewed earlier, you have all of the ingredients through engagement data, sentiment, and website analytics. What you need to do is cook up meaningful metric recipes to help measure what really matters.

Here are some simplified measurement ideas aligned around the most common business objectives discussed in this book.

- **Branding:** When it comes to measuring the impact of your brand-building efforts, you need to focus on metrics that demonstrate your growing reach and influence. Utilize website analytics such as visitors (especially new vs. returning—new traffic should go up as you increase brand awareness) and how much traffic is referred to your site from digital channels. You'll also want to look at social media metrics such as your "share of voice" compared to your competition (number of mentions of your brand vs. your industry mentions in your market or trade area as a whole). If used appropriately, your Klout score can also be a useful measurement of your brand's influence. (More on Klout and influence in a bit.)

- **Community building:** If building an engaged online community is your goal, you'll want to consider engagement data, but you'll also want to monitor the number of interactions among your community members. On your blog, podcast, or videos you'll want to keep track of your subscriptions, comments, reviews, and participation levels.

- **Public relations:** As noted earlier in this chapter, more mentions isn't always a good thing when evaluating your brand's social PR efforts. You'll want to also consider sentiment to get a gauge not only on how much you're being talked about, but whether it's positive or negative. Anyone can get mentions and coverage online today. It's context that matters more than ever.

- **Market research:** When it comes to new ideas you're able to glean from social media and digital marketing, it gets a little trickier to quantify using engagement data and website analytics alone. You'll have more success by co-opting methods you currently use in your organization to account for new product development and research costs. If new products are successful, the proof will be in the sales figures. Competitive insights gained can also help direct your efforts, which can result in cost savings that you can count toward the success of your digital market research.

- **Customer service:** Our final two destinations—customer service and lead generation/sales—make it easier by coming with legacy systems for tracking measurement and performance. When it comes to customer service, we have a history of meaningful metrics, including number of incidents, number of resolutions, and other data from customer relationship management (CRM) systems. The trick here is to tie your social customer service to the rest of your customer service operations, such as your call center. When you consider these metrics holistically you can also observe decreases in issues across other channels as more people take advantage of social customer service.

— **Lead generation/sales:** Your CRM data can also help you track leads and sales through the various online stages of your funnel. Offline, businesses can ask visitors "how did you hear about us?" and create social-media-only offers to drive in-store traffic. Those redeeming the offer can help you see social media's impact on sales online or off.

By boiling down the big data you're surrounded by, you can identify objective-based outcomes or key performance indicators (KPIs). While this may sound simple, it's something many marketers continue to struggle with. Data from Altimeter Group shows us that marketers' biggest challenge is the "inability to tie social media to business outcomes."[5] This is often a result of not having a business objective identified on the front end of your marketing strategy. In order to measure your impact, you must first know what it is you are trying to impact.

When we discussed identifying your business objective or destination back in Chapter 2, I told you about Scratch Cupcakery and the social-only offers they use to drive (and often double) in-store traffic. This simply defined business objective also easily connects itself to the metrics that matter. *Did this offer actually drive store traffic (leads) and sell more cupcakes (sales)?*

However, Scratch owner Natalie Brown cautions that measurement continues even after the special offer is redeemed at the door.

"Measuring the success of these posts is much more long-term than the post itself. We generally can't measure the success of a single post, but we can look at a week or a month and see what we've posted that has brought the most feedback. Customer interaction is really important, because that in itself boosts a post."[6]

You might also benefit from identifying additional scrappy metrics of your own. Publisher Penguin Group hosts Twitter Book Clubs with the hopes of driving sales of the titles discussed. However, it's challenging for them to identify books that are sold as a result of being mentioned on the Twitter chat as opposed to titles that are selling well on their own. Penguin's solution was to promote books during the Twitter chat using links to their own online store, which isn't trafficked much when compared with the sales being driven through Amazon and Barnes and Noble. As such, it's safe for them to conclude that any spikes in sales of select titles coming in through the online store are likely results of the Twitter Book Clubs.

With smart strategy as your foundation, it's easy to see your successes among the many numbers at your fingertips. Remember, it's not the size of the data, it's what you do with it.

AN ASIDE ON INFLUENCE

Earlier I mentioned using Klout as a meaningful metric when it comes to measuring branding. First, thank you for not chucking the book out the window or angrily tweeting how superficial I am for suggesting that Klout has some value. If you're surprised by my tone, you probably haven't brought up Klout in a room full of marketers. Many roll their eyes and sigh audibly when people make a reference to Klout, the (self-proclaimed) online standard of influence.

While it's true that Klout can be gamed (as most things online can) and has been misused by employers and marketers alike who have been known to occasionally require minimum Klout scores for jobs and special offers, it can be a useful ingredient in the metric recipes outlined previously. If you look beyond the hype, Klout measures how consistently and effectively you create content, conversations, and community. To raise your score, in a very broad sense, you would have to be working at doing all three of these things on a regular basis.

If anyone understands Klout's potential, it's Mark W. Schaefer, executive director of Schaefer Marketing Solutions and author of *Return on Influence*, the first book to explore the power of Klout. "The ability to create and move content is the absolute key to online influence. To the extent that you could actually measure that, wouldn't you also be creating an indicator of relative influence? That's what Klout is trying to do," offers Schaefer, who advises select clients to use Klout for measurement in certain situations. "To drive this metric up, brands have to do the work, and, in my view, it is the right kind of work."[7]

Schaefer also recommends using Klout as a scrappy monitoring tool by sorting your Twitter lists by Klout score using a tool like HootSuite. "This is a handy way to see which customers, competitors, and community members are doing the best job moving their content."[8] This can inform your engagement and help you identify influential community members, as discussed in Chapter 6.

Klout is also a simple and accessible metric on a scale of 1 to 100 that most understand, even at a very basic level. That makes it easy for your internal stakeholders to follow along. Some might even have a bit of fun monitoring your organization's Klout score. While it's not a panacea, Klout has the potential to be a scrappy metric that can help us track our progress and influence in creating content, conversations, and community online.

HOW DID YOU HEAR ABOUT US:
THE MYTH OF THE LAST IMPRESSION

One of the most tried-and-true means of learning what's actually moving the needle and bringing new people to your business offline, is asking one of the oldest questions in the book: *How did you hear about us?* This age-old question often comes with a supplied list of options (referral, search, TV ad, etc.) that you can modify to include your social media and content marketing.

For example, Park Nicollet, a nonprofit healthcare network headquartered in St. Louis Park, Minnesota, has made this question a part of their new patient intake form. At the smaller end of the spectrum, my dentist does the same thing. If a calendar is one of the scrappiest execution tools we can use, then a basic tally sheet next to the phone or at the front desk is one of the simplest measurement tools. Of course, these forms don't have to be low-tech either. You can also build this prompt into your CRM as you bring new leads and contacts into your system.

One complicating factor that emerges as we examine what's working and what's not in our marketing mix is the Myth of the Last Impression. This phenomenon simply means that when customers are asked to identify what led them into the store or to make their purchase, they often cite the last brand impression they experienced when, in reality, what moved them to action was really several brand impressions working in concert over time, leading up to that moment.

Branding is an experience that is a sum total of many parts, not a finite, linear path where a sale always occurs after a set point. This gets back to our continuous discussion on the changing nature of marketing today. That instant ding of the cash register has been replaced with longer-tail sales at the end of a long and winding relationship between you and your customers. As a result, measurement is compounded and cluttered. What really did move the needle?

This is not to say that you should throw measurement out with the bathwater. Rather, you need to look for a more holistic and focused means of measurement. Instead of asking the standard "how did you hear about us?" with a list of media options where just one lucky winner is checked (usually that last impression), perhaps customers should be allowed to select which combination of media and touch points inspired them to act. *Select all that apply* or *rate all that drove you to take action*.

As you work to understand the key touch points throughout your relationship with your customers, you can better craft an integrated and meaningful brand experience. We'll talk more about that in our final chapter. Now let's take a look at how you can demonstrate the success of your marketing with the rest of your team.

SIMPLIFYING MEASUREMENT AS A TEAM

Embracing your people power has been a big theme of this book, which continues here with measurement. Whether it's training your frontline staff to capture customer questions or working with them on important metrics you might measure, you need to bring your team into the fold. Once again, communication is key. They can't help you unless you fill them in on what it is you're trying to do and how you hope to measure it.

Don't laugh, but measurement can be fun. People like to see what's working and what's not. If you invite them into the process they can help you in ways you might not have imagined. One idea for sharing your successes is to come up with a simple scorecard you can share with the team. Because the data and analytics all of these robust systems spit out can be daunting and inaccessible, you can help communicate key metrics and successes by distilling all of this down into a simple one-page report you can share with management and select team members.

Start by planning a basic Word document and split it into a table with either six cells (two columns, three rows) or eight cells (two columns, four rows). In each cell include a data point you're watching and why. Make it a mix of objective-based relevant recipes as noted earlier, as well as some fun qualitative items. Here are some ideas on data points you might include on your scorecard:

— **Key social metrics such as "share of voice":** Select one of your leading objective-based outcomes discussed earlier. For these first two metrics you share, clearly restate how they help you reach your defined destination (*example:* 40 percent share of voice for local banking conversations vs. 34 percent last month).

— **Key website metrics such as new visitors vs. returning or average time on site:** Again, tie this metric to a destination the rest of the team knows you're working to reach.

— **Follower/like counts:** While these numbers don't matter the most, they are metrics that a majority of people understand and can identify with. Keeping track of your overall reach can be fun for others to observe.

— **Mentions with or without sentiment metrics:** Whether or not you include sentiment depends on your marketing objective. While insightful, sentiment can get pricey as most tools that include this advanced metric are quite expensive and intended for larger, enterprise-level use. Again, measure only what matters for *you*.

— **Top content:** Sharing the top three most trafficked blog posts over the past month helps your team, especially your blog authors, know what's getting traction and what they can help you create more of. It can also help spark new ideas for new forms of content and other customer experience innovations.

— **Klout score:** This metric provides a nice "quality score" to your marketing.

— **Customer story/tweet of the month:** Again, it's nice to have some qualitative insights here too. What stories are you hearing from customers? Was there a neat Facebook comment or customer tweet? As marketers we hear this feedback all the time, but others in your organization might be starving for these real-life stories.

— **Instagram photo of the month:** More of the same. Though this might not be a measurement per se, it helps your team "see" the results of your work as well.

With your scorecard mapped out in Word or something similar, you can easily grab screenshots of various dashboards from Google Analytics, Facebook Insights, Klout, and more. Once you have a format you and your team like, it won't take much for you to update this each month. While we'd like to believe that everyone reads the multipage reports we send out each month, you'll find that the scorecard approach will be more effective at bringing your team in sync with what you're working on.

Remember, the more your team knows the more they can help you. (You should consider making this your marketing mantra! It's certainly one of my favorites.)

THE BOTTOM LINE IN SIMPLIFYING MEASUREMENT

At a SXSW session about social media ROI, a panel of industry experts engaged in a lively discussion on the challenges and merits of measurement. As the conversation died down for a moment, panelist Matt Ridings, head of market innovation at CrowdSource, quietly offered a new thought: "Don't we make all of this [ROI] too hard?" Ridings has a point. We've been struggling to tie our marketing to measurable outcomes since Montgomery Ward and the first direct-response ads they ran. Some forms of media work better than others.

Above all, we must resist the temptation to overcomplicate measurement and ROI. While it is indeed a challenging task, we need to remember the Altimeter data showing that the biggest struggle comes from the fact that we can't tie our marketing back to a measurable business objective.[9] What are we trying to do with our marketing in the first place? If we know this, we'll be on the right track once it's time to measure.

We also need to consider other ways of approaching the impact of our efforts as well. Ford has identified one such metric. Global Vice President of Marketing and Sales Jim Farley notes that when you compare new media efforts to the big brand TV ads they traditionally ran, "We can lower the amount of traditional advertising we do and see massive cost savings. We spend 10 cents on the dollar."[10] Farley can't get at the direct result of social media on car sales, given the complexity of the automotive distribution channel. Instead of wringing his hands, he points to savings they can see through doing less mass media advertisements and focusing on social media to drive the same amount of awareness, excitement, and leads to their dealer network.

Speaking of traditional media and measurement, it's also worth noting for just a moment the intense scrutiny we subject new media to is not always visited upon our broadcast media counterparts. While we can get close to an accurate assessment of digital ROI, it's still imperfect. However, this measurement is much more precise than any number traditional media can deliver. We know that an impression is an impression and a click is a click. Those are actions that have actually happened and, therefore, can be accurately counted.

Are we suggesting that we cry about this? Not at all. But let's call it out for what it is and point to the simplified successes that we can isolate and measure.

THE REAL POINT OF MEASUREMENT

Because we exert so much effort on the act of measurement itself, it's easy to lose sight of why we care about it in the first place. Sure, it's important to know if what we just did actually accomplished what it was supposed to, but it's also important as we look ahead and work on the next marketing map we create. Or perhaps a refinement of the one we just executed. The single most important thing after identifying a KPI is knowing what you plan on doing with the data you've gathered. Again, numbers aren't hard to come by in digital marketing. In addition to finding the metrics that matter most, you need to focus what actions you'll take as a result of what you learn along the way.

As you read your results, don't forget the advice conveyed to me by my direct marketing mentor, former publishing executive and consultant Peter Bergen, who said that in marketing, "a clear failure is as useful as a clear success."[11] Even after a failure, you still know one more thing that doesn't work, so you can focus your marketing even more in the future. Beyond being meaningful, make sure that your data points provide you with the opportunity to be decisive as well.

Planning, executing, measuring, and iterating are the path to continuous improvement in marketing. Do this by first getting smart and planning your work. Then get scrappy as you work the plan. Finally, as you gain experience with the plan, you can begin to simplify it—with even better outcomes.

And now that you've added appropriate metrics to the mix, you get to start the whole process all over again.

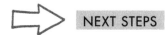 **NEXT STEPS**

Take your next steps toward more meaningful measurement by answering the following questions.

- List some of the metrics you're currently using to measure your digital marketing. Remember, these metrics usually come in three categories:

    - Engagement data

    - Sentiment

    - Website analytics

- How can you use this data to cook up meaningful metric

recipes around the core objectives outlined in your marketing map?

— How can you create an easy-to-follow digital scorecard to
share with your team? Which quantitative and qualitative
metrics could you include?

— What improvements can you make as the result of more
meaningful measurement?

Chapter 9

PUTTING IT TOGETHER

Now what? We've simplified our social media and our content marketing. We have a system for measuring what matters, which can help us simplify our digital marketing even further. But where do we go from here?

In Chapter 6, I referenced the painter Georges Seurat as we learned to connect our digital dots. Stephen Sondheim's 1984 musical *Sunday in the Park with George* offers a fictional account of the artist and the characters who form the real-life painting *A Sunday Afternoon on the Island of La Grande Jatte*. Act II of the musical features a song about the art of making art called "Putting It Together," whose lyrics point out that in a work of art, "Every moment makes a contribution/Every little detail plays a part."[1] In the end, though, as the song reminds us, putting it all together is what really counts.

Sondheim's lyrics inform your next scrappy marketing steps as well. You have to put it all together, bit by bit. To do so, you must take a step back and consider your entire brand experience from your customer's perspective. Every little detail plays a part. In addition to connecting your digital dots online, how can you connect the rest of your marketing dots?

- - -

While the scrappy approach is designed to help you utilize today's digital marketing tools, what you do offline is a part of your overall brand experience as well. When your touch points are developed harmoniously, you have the perfect realization of the modern gestalt brand, where the whole is indeed more than the sum of any individual parts. That's why you need to focus on putting it all together if you want to make sure your marketing counts.

At the end of the day, this is the skill that best defines the scrappy marketer. The ability to see the bigger picture among isolated tactical steps and vice versa is more important to your success than deep experience in a particular marketing discipline, media, or technology. This ability informs your role in crafting and communicating a unified brand experience, the primary focus of this final chapter.

We'll also recap the scrappy marketing system, going over each of the key points covered throughout this book. We'll close with a big-picture look at why this framework matters, and pose some final next steps for your own marketing journey.

Let's begin by taking a look at how you can make the whole of your marketing more than the sum of its parts.

SOME FINAL DIGITAL DOTS WORTH CONNECTING

We covered integration among the primary digital brand touch points of email marketing and POEM (paid, owned, earned, media) back in Chapter 6, but now let's look at a few more scrappy digital dots we can connect.

Remember how you need to embrace your people power? And the fact that 75 percent of us prefer to receive marketing messages via email?[2] Make sure you ask each of your employees to include your brand's social media links in their corporate email signatures as well. Digital signatures are the perfect example of dots that are easy to forget. Remind your team members to include links to your social outposts or your latest content. Or both.

Your website itself should feature prominent social linkage as well. If possible, don't just tile the icons arbitrarily. Tell the members of your community what they can expect to gain by connecting with you. Don't hide your blog posts, podcasts, and other new forms of content either. Your latest content can't live up to its full potential if you bury it on your website. One scrappy tactic for calling out your most important content is through a WordPress plug-in like Hello Bar, which adds a simple text-based bar at the top of your website with a call-to-action link. This can be useful for a new e-book, podcast, or other announcements.

Your website should be the very hub of your online ecosystem and social brand experience. Too often, marketers treat the homepage as a sacred monolith, banishing social content rather than putting it front and center to provide an inviting point of entry.

With all of your digital touch points under control, are you ready to take a look at what you can do offline?

CONNECTING THE REST OF YOUR MARKETING

While we've focused heavily on digital channels, most marketers have other forms of media working hard for them as well. How can you better integrate your non-digital channels with what you're doing online? As noted in Chapter 6, integration is more than simply slapping the social media icons at the end of your TV commercial or on the back of your latest brochure. It's easy to fall into this routine. In fact, I'd wager that if you look up from this book right now you can probably see the ubiquitous Facebook and Twitter logos somewhere nearby.

Does that mean you shouldn't use these icons? Of course not. Instead, make sure you pair these icons with a call to action reminding potential fans of what they can expect to find when they take the time to connect with you. Before I could wag my finger at my local Hy-Vee grocery store, the employee-owned supermarket chain switched from basic hand-drawn signage of a big lonely Facebook icon to a larger banner inviting customers to "stay connected with your Coralville Hy-Vee and view our special offers and upcoming events!" This is a great example of making a social call to action sharp and specific. Bravo, Hy-Vee! Way to go!

As the father of five children, going to the dentist's office is major event. Since my wife gave birth to the kids, I figured the least I could do was take care of this chore every six months. You could say that while sitting in the dentist's office waiting (and adding up in my head how much all of this will cost), I'm something of a captive audience. I'm also thinking about my kids' teeth and preventative care more than usual. Dr. Don Peterson of the Iowa Pediatric Dental Center takes advantage of my time (and captivity) to promote ways for connecting with his practice online via various social networks through signage in the waiting area. Instead of just displaying the bare logos in front of me, the practice includes a brief sentence outlining what kind of conversations and content I can find on each platform. Maybe I will connect on YouTube if there are educational videos that will keep my kids from just running their toothbrushes under the water!

Where can you connect these dots? This answer is simple too. Everywhere.

Key Offline Touch Points for Digital Integration

Here's a quick touch point list to make sure that your entire brand experience is connected with your digital ecosystem:

- In-store signage/point-of-sale materials

- On-hold messages

- Product packaging: boxes, bags, sacks, etc.

- Marketing collateral: brochures and flyers

- Receipts

- Business cards and letterhead

- Vehicles

Marketing Channels for Digital Integration

How about your other marketing channels? You need to connect them as well.

- **Broadcast media:** TV, radio, and print audiences should be told how they can connect online to learn more.

- **Direct marketing/mail:** Again, more than just icons.

- **Public relations:** Be sure your media releases and online brand center have links to your social media channels and content resources.

- **Personal sales and customer service:** These frontline team members are already getting social with your customers offline.

- **Trade show/exhibit materials:** If you connect with people at live events, make it easy for them to connect with you online.

Online Touch Points for Digital Integration

And here's a quick overview of digital touch points you need to consider and connect as well.

- Website

- Email marketing (and employee signatures)

- Paid search advertising

- Social media advertising

- Online display advertising

- Online radio advertising (Pandora, Spotify ads)

- Earned media: guest posts and other off-site outposts

- Social media profiles: include links to your other social sites

If this sounds like a lot of work, you're right. In fact, it could sound like an entirely new job. Instead, you should think of it as a new way of thinking about your current job.

YOUR NEW JOB

When working with the City of Newton, Iowa, on a rebranding project for the community, I was charged with presenting the new system to the public at a large pep rally. To close the event, the city's mayor took the stage and asked the audience to raise their right hands and repeat after him. It was then that he swore in each and every one of them as official Newton brand ambassadors.

While your charge may not be as legally binding as the mayor's, it should be taken just as seriously. In fact, in most cases, you will be the chief brand ambassador, responsible for setting your brand strategy in motion and deputizing the rest of your team (another example of embracing your people power). While some bystanders take their view of this role to the militant extreme, referring to internal stewards as "the brand police," it's your job to make sure that all of your communications internally and externally are on-brand.

The "brand police" nickname is usually applied when those not connected to branding and marketing confuse this kind of commitment on your part with your being a control freak. What they don't understand is the gestalt principle at play in our marketing today. Though the whole is more than the sum of the parts, it's hard to keep an eye on the whole when the parts cut across a variety of departments internally. After a quick scan of your brand, you'll realize that these touch points exist in product design and development, distribution, logistics, and more.

It would be easy to keep your head down and not risk traveling into dicey cross-departmental waters. However, the scrappy marketer also understands that everything works better when the message is unified. Does the copy in a shipping email really make or break your branding? Again, you could simply stay out of this and let your customer service and distribution teams handle it. But then you'd miss another opportunity to communicate who you are and to deepen your customer relationship. That's exactly what Warby Parker does with their email confirmations once your glasses try-on-at-home order has shipped, which humorously opens with the subject line, "Let the obsessive package tracking begin."

How do you get started with this enormous undertaking? Start with a simple audit of your brand experience from your customer's perspective, beginning with how people first encounter your brand (online, offline, or both) all the way through the sales process to how the relationship is nurtured after the sale. During your journey, you'll want to diagnose holes in your message coverage and recommend fixes to the responsible departments.

Every detail matters from the customer's perspective. The sad fact of the matter is that many people in your organization probably lack the ability to see the whole. Will you take advantage of each and every opportunity? If so, then it's time for you to raise your right hand and get sworn in.

CREATING AN ACTIVE COMMUNITY

The bigger opportunity you can realize from bringing together all of your marketing touch points is to more effectively involve your offline community in your online conversations. The difference between slapping social media icons onto your offline touch points and being prescriptive is really the difference between having a passive and active community.

Team Chevy, the official NASCAR racing arm of Chevrolet, could have easily checked the integration box off of their list with standard social media icon signs during their exhibit of vehicles that accompanies the racing circuit tour. After a quick glance at their signs, it could seem like that's exactly what they did. However, a closer inspection shows that they've actually used the signs next to the vehicles to direct people to their social channels to "share their Team Chevy experience." They even spell out their usernames or handles on various social networks, making it easy for people to find them. Isn't the goal of having a car on display to spark conversations? This simple instruction encourages fans to do this both online and offline.

Ragstock, a Minneapolis-based chain that specializes in secondhand or "recycled clothing," uses Instagram to employ a similar strategy. Trying on clothes is a social experience offline, right? Why not connect this conversation online as well? A series of simple in-store signs direct customers to tag #ragstock on Instagram for a chance to win a gift card. They've not only encouraged online conversations offline, they've rewarded them. The result? Thousands of in-store selfies tagged with their brand.

In addition to sparking conversations, you can also use in-store signage to drive user-generated content online—such as social updates and selfies—which you can turn around and use offline as well. That's exactly what American Eagle Outfitters did. Customer selfies were tiled together to cover entire windows of their retail stores. Included among these panels was the hashtag #AEO, which helped drive more user-generated content online as the cycle continued.

Taken to the extreme, you can create your whole offline experience based on online content. The 1888 Hotel in Sydney, Australia, uses Instagram photos from guests and travelers to decorate the walls and common areas throughout their 90-room boutique hotel. Using the hashtag #1888hotel, guests can see a continuously updated feed of photos on screens at reception. They also have a special "selfie space" where guests can have fun behind a gilt frame.

Heavy online users are rewarded offline as well. Those with over 10,000 followers get a free night's stay, as does the guest who takes the most creative photo each month. More than a social network that supports their business, Instagram activity is a unique aspect of the 1888 Hotel's overall brand experience. It's hard to tell where the marketing starts and stops and where the customer experience begins. This is the very definition of a total brand experience that transcends and integrates all online and offline touch points.

When Alan Mulally took the reins at Ford Motor Company in 2006, he implemented his famous One Ford strategy. This helped the automaker—once weighed down with extraneous product lines, brands, and a host of challenges—retake control of its own destiny. One Ford unified its team, plan, and goal. This simplicity and focus had a ripple effect on all things at Ford, including social media and digital marketing. "It certainly made my job a lot easier," said Scott Monty, Ford's former global head of social media who has gone on to found Scott Monty Strategies. "Alan's spirit of transparency, collaboration, and accountability was directly applicable to what the social media team was trying to accomplish, and with a CEO who led by example, it demonstrated the importance of working together."[3]

Are you the CEO of an auto manufacturer? Statistically speaking, probably not. But remember, the scrappy marketer sees ideas everywhere. As diffused as marketing is getting, you could take a page from Mulally's playbook for unifying things at Ford. You need to bring your marketing together strategically in pursuit of a singular focus.

As media has evolved rapidly over the past decade, digital initiatives grew up separately alongside the rest of marketing. As digital continues to mature, we run the risk of siloed marketing. Digital marketing and the "other stuff." Maintaining these separate entities is neither smart, scrappy, nor particularly simple. Having two or more marketing systems internally is a perfect example of marketing that is more complex than it needs to be. When you're supporting two systems it's hardly as effective or efficient as it could be, so it certainly isn't scrappy. But the biggest red flag is that's it's not smart.

By bringing everything you do to market your organization together, you'll truly be able to do more with less and create smarter digital marketing.

A SCRAPPY RECAP

Scrappy marketing is no small task. Along the way I've asked you to think about new things and to think differently about things you're already doing. Because of the comprehensive nature of all of this, let's take a moment to review the key ideas laid out in *Get Scrappy*.

Smart Steps You Can't Skip

Though the marketing megaphone has changed in recent years with the rise of digital channels like Facebook, Twitter, and Instagram, as well as the increased importance of content marketing, the fundamentals behind that megaphone remain the same. You have to build a strong, clear, and consistent brand now more than ever if you want to get the most from your marketing.

Remember the five-step brand blueprint process. Your brand must have these unique features:

- Spark

- Promise

- Story

- Voice

- Visuals

To avoid being like Alice in Wonderland, not sure where you're going or which path to take, you have to have a plan. Instead of over-thinking this process through massive internal efforts, consider the metaphor of the map. Your plan will lead you to your desired destination and help you find your way if you are lost. The most common marketing destinations or business objectives include:

- Branding

- Community building

- Public relations

- Market research

- Customer service

- Lead generation and sales

Avoid getting lost among the Shiny New Things by using the points on your digital compass to determine what channels work best when.

Do More with Less

With mousetrap marketing that is more effective and efficient you can topple the Myth of Big (only big brands with big budgets can do big things). Here's how you can do more with less:

- **Create a question engine.** This will help you develop a sustainable system for creating conversations and content online. The questions you ask can spark conversations on social networks, while the questions you answer through blog posts, videos, podcasts, and more will help you help your customers and provide value to your community.

— **Embrace your people power.** Turn your people problem around! How to staff marketing is one of the biggest obstacles in your path today. With your leadership and guidance, your people can be your single greatest asset. Look to examples of marketers doing big things with scrappy teams. Like Ben and Jerry's and New Belgium Brewing, find ways you can creatively divide both your team and your work.

— **Connect your digital dots.** You need to bring everything together online to get scrappy with your digital marketing. Make sure that your new channels include your legacy systems like email marketing, paid search and social media advertising, as well as your earned media efforts. You need to tie together all pieces of the POEM (paid, owned, and earned media) when it comes to your marketing.

Simplify for the Long Haul

As you put your marketing in motion, you have to be on the lookout for ways to further simplify your work. Your first step is acknowledging the fact that marketers at times make marketing more complex than it needs to be, often under the guise of continuous improvement (more meetings, more plans, more forms, etc.). You can simplify your content creation by grounding your work with strategy and employing four helpful content creation hacks:

— Relentlessly repurposing content

- Utilizing historical content

- Curating content

- Encouraging user-generated content

Simplifying your social media conversations starts by focusing on the right things. We spend an excessive amount of time on what could go wrong conversationally now that the audience can talk back. Instead you need to focus on the bigger issue of building strong relationships with your most excited fans and developing strategies for transforming them into social brand ambassadors.

It's easier to simplify your marketing when you measure what matters. This will help eliminate things that aren't working and amplify the things that are. There's no shortage of metrics in digital marketing today. That's why you need to develop recipes for success grounded in the strategies and objectives laid out in your marketing map.

As we just learned, the scrappy marketer also knows that the whole is more than the sum of its parts. The greatest approach to marketing simplification is to unify your entire brand experience from your customer's perspective. Discovering how all of your touch points—both online and off—work together to create your brand is critical in getting the most from your marketing.

- - - - - - - - - - - - -
A RELIABLE, REPEATABLE
FRAMEWORK FOR WHAT'S NEXT

While it could seem as though we've focused heavily on social media and content marketing, my intention wasn't to merely create another digital marketing book for the latest Shiny New Things. Rather, the scrappy approach introduces a reliable and repeatable framework you can use for whatever lies ahead. What's next isn't always clear. One thing that's obvious is that brands won't be getting any *less* social anytime soon.

The scrappy mindset—putting brains before budget, marketing effectively and efficiently like a mousetrap, and seeing ideas everywhere—can help you manage any new platform or content opportunity that arises in the future. From here, you can get smart with strategy, do more with less, and simplify your work for the long haul. This provides a framework for reinventing marketing as marketing reinvents itself.

While all of this technology is powerful, it's important to remember that social media and digital marketing are a means and not an end. Facebook, Twitter, Instagram, and other new and exciting forms of content are merely the tools you can use to take advantage of the other, amazing opportunity available today: building close, personal relationships with your customers and community. Outside of a small town retail context, where a shopkeeper usually knew all of their customers by name, getting close with your constituents had largely been outmoded by mass media and the "bigger is better" mentality discussed in this book. But now personal connections and human interactions are coming back in a big way. Seeing past the Shiny New Things to this opportunity is what you need to embrace.

You can personally answer customers' questions in real time or near real time via Twitter and take them behind the scenes of your business and new products through videos and blog posts. You have the potential to connect in a more human way than ever before. Don't get caught up in the excitement of the tools. Look beyond the shiny for new ways to use these platforms to deepen your relationships with the people who matter most—your customers, potential customers, and your community at large.

These digital tools provide opportunities to surprise and delight, to go above and beyond. However, a new norm is fast approaching that you can't ignore as you look ahead.

THE NEW NORM HAS RAISED THE BAR

The new norm is that there isn't a norm. Rather, there isn't a status quo. Remember the challenge of Checklist Marketing? Arbitrarily checking marketing channels off of lists so we can feel like we're "doing it all" regardless of whether or not a particular platform makes sense. We do this because we want to be caught up. *When will we be done with all of this digital marketing stuff? How much is enough? When can we set it and forget it?*

You aren't going to like my answer. The fact of the matter is that these aren't simple boxes that you can check off on some list. Technology and new media are changing at an unprecedented pace and don't show any signs of slowing down. In addition to making marketers dizzy trying to keep up with the rapid pace of change, it's also changing consumer behavior and expectations. The cold, hard truth is this: Change is the new norm and the bar has been raised.

You may have set up outposts on every social network under the sun, but what if a customer actually has a real problem? In real time? How do you respond? On a recent family vacation, we made reservations at several Hilton properties on our way to Cape Cod. On our first night we were thrown a curve when our reservation had not been booked for the night we had requested. (I remember making the reservation for Friday the 13th—one doesn't forget this ominous, unlucky date when locking it down for a big family road trip.)

Despite being Hilton Honors members, we were let down by

poor customer service at the desk and on the phone. I took to Twitter and was direct-messaged. An hour later. The social media honeymoon ended quickly with an impersonal message to call their customer service 800-number, which I had already unsuccessfully done. It's not enough to just plant a flag on social media. You have to create a timely, human experience there. Not just a redirect to your other channels.

We are creating more content than ever before—blog posts, e-books, videos, podcasts, webinars, and more. However, according to data from SiriusDecisions, between 60 and 70 percent of the content we create goes unused.[4] It isn't enough to just turn your content creation up to 11 (that's for all of you *Spinal Tap* fans out there). You have to create better, more relevant content than ever before. Especially if you want your brand's content to overcome "content shock," Mark W. Schaefer's idea that we first explored in Chapter 7, reminding us that content supply will eventually exceed audience demand.[5]

Everything discussed here is further accentuated by the proliferation of mobile and wearable technology. "The mobile moment" described by Tim Hayden and Tom Webster in their book *The Mobile Commerce Revolution* provides brands with opportunities for unprecedented relevance.[6] And yet many businesses' mobile strategy is nothing more than encouraging people to check in on Facebook, Foursquare, or Swarm.

What are you offering them in this moment beyond a passive "cold check-in"? It isn't enough to just ask someone to check in. You have to find some way of making this act worth your guest's while. Are they having a birthday? Send them an e-card. Is it their first visit? Send them a coupon. Focus on the variety of ways you can celebrate and seize the mobile moment.

Nothing is slowing down. Nothing is getting any easier. The bar has indeed been raised and that is the new norm. You have to commit more of your time, talent, and treasure to more than just understanding these new digital tools. You have to rethink your marketing and how you can provide a more meaningful, relevant, and timely experience.

How will you clear this new bar?

WHY BETTER MARKETING MATTERS

When I deliver keynotes at conferences, I often wrap up by saying that better marketers create a better world. Am I a little biased on the subject? You bet! I spend 100 percent of my non-family time focused on marketing, specifically consulting, coaching, speaking, and teaching marketers and future marketers. Oh, and I'm also a marketer myself.

Bias aside, I truly believe that better marketers create a better world. Why? Because better marketers create better marketing. While marketing is the principal export of our industry it ends up helping us all too. Marketing works to promote profitable exchanges in goods and services across all sectors—from solo entrepreneurs to small businesses, from global corporations to nonprofits. All of these organizations require marketing. Of course, not all of them know this, but that's a topic for another book.

Better marketers create better marketing, which in turn yields a better world for several reasons. First, effective marketing allows every kind of organization to grow and prosper. As our communities are made up of a variety of different types of institutions, it's easy to see how better marketers and marketing create stronger businesses and better communities. All of this adds up to economic growth and innovation from the local level to the global economy. It's not hard to see the impact better marketers can have on the world.

Effective marketing also creates a more pleasant world. When practiced properly, marketing aligns products, services, and other offerings with customers' specific needs. This leads to marketing messages and promotions similarly tailored to relevant audience segments. In theory, when marketing is better, you shouldn't be bombarded with irrelevant messages and pointless offers.

This brings me to my final point. That's the fact that there's never been a better time to be in marketing. To some, this is a scary time as the very foundation of how we communicate with customers is being rocked by the changes brought about by the Internet and various forms of social media and digital marketing. However, it's also an exciting time. The better marketing outlined here—defined by close, direct relationships with your customers—requires a better form of communication and new tools. That's exactly what the digital revolution has brought us.

Your customers aren't miles away, accessible only through focus groups and industry trade shows. Today they're just a few clicks away on your Facebook page, Twitter profile, or Instagram feed. You don't have to be intrusive and interrupt the wrong audience anymore. Through today's marketing tools you can connect with interested people who want to hear from you and build relationships over time.

These tools make better marketing possible. And yet many are content to keep their heads in the sand, interrupting the wrong people with their marketing, while complaining about the commercials during their favorite shows and the advertisements above urinals. Or, worse still, there are those marketers who persist in using today's tools like the mass media tools of the past.

Marketing can be a noble profession. It can lead to better communities locally and across the globe. What will you do? Will you help make the world better or continue interrupting people with your head in the sand?

NEXT STEPS: JOURNEY'S END?

My goal with *Get Scrappy* was to arm you with a reliable and repeatable framework for rethinking your marketing at one of the most exciting times to be a marketer. The core concepts of putting your brains before your budget, marketing like a mousetrap, and seeing ideas everywhere will help you create smarter digital marketing for your business, overcoming those common obstacles—the Myth of Big, Shiny New Things, and Checklist Marketing. Now you know how to get smart, do more with less, and simplify your work for the long haul, regardless of which tools and technologies are in the headlines.

Remember, the Urban Dictionary defines *scrappy* as referring to "someone or something that appears dwarfed by a challenge, but more than compensates for seeming inadequacies through will, persistence, and heart."[7] These traits are also the defining attributes of the scrappy marketer. Through your will, persistence, and heart, you can tackle the challenges you face and transform them into opportunities to build your brand and grow your business.

While this may be the end of the book, it's by no means the end of our journey. We scrappy marketers have to stick together! At GetScrappyBook.com you'll find resources related to the book as well as opportunities for you to share your scrappy stories or other scrappy examples you find out in the wild to help us all continue to see ideas everywhere. We're all part of the scrappy marketing community now. Keep the conversation going online using the hashtag #GetScrappy.

And finally, speaking of close personal relationships fostered by digital technology, I want to build one with you. Feel free to email me your questions, ideas, and insights on the book. My email address is nick@westergaard.com (my first name @ my last name dot com—how's that for simple?). You can also connect with me on most social networks by searching for the username @nickwestergaard.

Let's take the next steps together.

APPENDIX

.

GET SCRAPPY:
A REFERENCE GUIDE

Are you ready to start getting scrappy? Here's a handy reference guide to help you implement this framework at your organization.

The Scrappy Mindset
- Brains Before Budget: Scrappy marketers always look before they leap.
- Market Like a Mousetrap: Be on the lookout for ways to be more effective and efficient with your marketing.
- See Ideas Everywhere: Technology today moves too fast to be confined by your industry or market when it comes to looking for ideas you can borrow in your work.

The Brand Behind the Megaphone
Strong brands with something to say matter more than ever in the digital age. Remember to create a brand with:

- Spark: Why does your brand exist?
- Promise: What do you do and for whom?
- Story: What's your brand's three-word story?

- - -

- Voice: How does that story sound?
- Visuals: How does that story come to life visually, online and off?

Share this brand blueprint with your team so everyone understands who you are and what you stand for.

Map Your Marketing

Don't get bogged down by strategy. Look for ways to create a digital marketing map to guide your work. Use Rudyard Kipling's "serving men" (why, what, when, where, who, and how) to help you get started. Like any map, you need a destination (the "why" in the Kipling model). Here are the most common destinations or business objectives we drive toward with our marketing.

- Branding
- Community building
- Public relations
- Market research
- Customer service
- Lead generation/sales

Choose one or two of these to focus on and create a map that is SMART:

- *Specific*
- *Measurable*
- *Attainable*
- *Relevant*
- *Time-related*

Follow Your Digital Compass

When it comes to determining what social media channels and content marketing formats you use when, be sure to align the *why* of your business objective (your destination) with the *who* of your audience. These two compass points will help point your marketing in the right direction.

Create a Question Engine

Make your ongoing digital marketing efforts more sustainable by helping your customers with your social media and content marketing. Use questions to fuel your content creation and to spark social media conversations.

- Collect a list of questions your customers have today. Think about how you can use these questions to create helpful content in the form of blog posts, videos, and podcasts.

- Start a list of questions you can ask your community via social media to keep your conversations moving and to feed your editorial calendar. Enlist your colleagues at the office in this task (see next topic).

Embrace Your People Power

Forget about your "people problems." Embrace your people power and put your biggest asset to work in your digital marketing. Like the examples from Ben & Jerry's and New Belgium Brewing, you need to find ways to get scrappy with your staffing both internally and externally. Remember, your people—both your team members and your community—won't know how to help you until you ask them.

Connect Your Digital Dots

Social media and content marketing are two of the more popular categories within digital marketing. To get scrappy, you have to connect these initiatives to classic digital channels such as email marketing and search-engine optimization. You also need to be mindful of POEM, managing the integration of your *p*aid, *o*wned, and *e*arned *m*edia.

Throughout all of your marketing you need to make sure that when you promote your channels, you do more than simply slap the social media icons onto things. Tell people why they should bother to connect with you.

The Simplification Game

To simplify your digital marketing for the long haul, implement these four content creation hacks to help you get the most from your marketing:

- Relentlessly repurpose content.
- Utilize historical content.
- Curate content.
- Encourage user-generated content.

Social media conversations can be simplified by focusing on the most important conversations. While you need a plan for negative customer interactions, you also need a plan for how to convert your positive customers into social brand ambassadors.

Measure What Matters

Metrics are abundant in digital marketing. Measure what matters by aligning your performance data around your map's destination or business objective. Use these metric recipes to help you share your success with the rest of your team.

Putting It Together

The whole is more than the sum of its parts. To create marketing that matters, you have to put everything together, creating a unified brand experience both online and off. By embracing your new role as chief brand ambassador and bringing together everything you do to market your organization, you'll be on your way to doing more with less and creating smarter digital marketing.

DISCUSSION GROUP QUESTIONS

If you read *Get Scrappy* with your team, bookgroup, or in a class-room, here are some questions to spark follow-up discussions on the ideas and frameworks presented in this book.

Introduction
- What are your biggest obstacles with social media and digital marketing?
- Are you distracted by Shiny New Things?
- Does the Myth of Big weigh you down?
- Do you succumb to Checklist Marketing?
- Are there other organizational obstacles you're working to overcome?

Chapter 1
- Do you have a clearly defined brand? Think about where you are today and where you want to be.
- Take turns sharing what your brand is and what you stand for.
- If your brand is less defined, how might you bring this into focus using the brand blueprint concept?

- - -

Chapter 2

- Does your social media and/or content marketing have a singular focus? Is it tied to an organizational objective?
- If not, review the six common destinations—branding, community building, public relations, market research, customer service, and lead generation/sales—and consider how you can ground your work around an objective or two.

Chapter 3

- Which social media channels are you currently using?
- Are they tied to your organizational objective(s)?
- How are they connected to your audience's unique needs?
- Are there channels you are using just for the sake of planting a flag there? If so, ask yourself if it's really worth your time and resources.

Chapter 4

- Are you answering your customers' questions?
- If not, how can you use their questions to spark social media conversations and fuel content such as blog posts, videos, and podcasts?

Chapter 5

- What's your organization's stance on employees and social media?
- Are your team members involved in your digital marketing or are they discouraged from even accessing these social networks?
- How can you get scrappy with your staffing by involving both your internal team members and your external customers and agency partners in your digital marketing efforts?

Chapter 6

- How does your social media and content marketing connect to the rest of your digital marketing such as email, search-engine optimization, and other forms of online advertising?
- If these channels are siloed, how can you better align your objectives, messaging, and measurement?
- Are there efficiencies you can realize by connecting these digital dots?

Chapter 7

- Are you getting more than one piece of content from everything you create? If not, how can you relentlessly repurpose? For example, could your blog post become a video? Could your e-book become a series of blog posts and an infographic?
- Are you utilizing historical content, curated content, and user-generated content? How can you make these scrappy content hacks a more consistent part of your marketing?
- How do you treat your best customers online? Do you have a plan for elevating them to social brand ambassadors—raving fans—who can help you down the road?

Chapter 8

- Are you measuring what matters most for your organization? Is it tied to your objective(s)?
- If not, how can you use metrics such as engagement data, sentiment, and website analytics to create recipes for measuring your social and digital success?

Chapter 9

— What does your brand experience look like from the customers' perspective? Are they seeing the big picture—a holistic, clear, consistent brand? Or are they seeing a fragmented brand, with different messages and touch points across different channels?

— How can you bring everything together, online and off, to create a whole that is more than the sum of its parts?

FURTHER READING

Get Scrappy covers a lot of different topics, many of which are explored in greater detail in other books. Here are just a few that are worth your time. Think of this as your scrappy reading list.

More on Branding
Primal Branding and *The Social Code* by Patrick Hanlon
Digital Branding by Daniel Rowles
Brand Against the Machine by John Michael Morgan

More on Digital Marketing
Youtility by Jay Baer
Optimize by Lee Odden
The Rebel's Guide to Email Marketing by Jason Falls and
  DJ Waldow

More on Content Marketing
Content Rules by Ann Handley and C.C. Chapman
The Content Code by Mark W. Schaefer

More on Social Media

The Art of Social Media by Guy Kawasaki and Peg Fitzpatrick
Likeable Social Media by Dave Kerpen

BONUS! More on Human Nature

To Sell Is Human by Daniel H. Pink
No One Understands You and What to Do About It by Heidi
     Grant Halvorson

NOTES

Introduction

1. "scrappy." Merriam-Webster.com/dictionary/scrappy, accessed July 21, 2015. http://www.merriam-webster.com.
2. "scrappy." Urban Dictionary, 2008, accessed July 21, 2015, http://www.urbandictionary.com.
3. Samantha Hersil (Digital Marketing Coordinator, Pacific Cycle), in discussion with the author, April 2015.
4. "Trying to build a better mousetrap," CBS Sunday Morning, accessed on July 21, 2015, http://www.cbsnews.com/news/trying-to-build-a-better-mousetrap/.
5. Jeremy Gutsche, interview by Mitch Joel, *Six Pixels of Separation,* Twist Image, May 10, 2015, http://www.twistimage.com/podcast/archives/spos-461—jeremy-gutsche-wants-you-to-be-better-and-faster/.
6. "Super Bowl ads: What could you buy for the cost of a commercial?," BBC News, accessed on July 21, 2015, http://www.bbc.com/news/world-us-canada-31064972.
7. "Anheuser-Busch Announces Super Bowl XLVIII Ad Lineup," BBC News, accessed on July 21, 2015, http://newsroom.anheuser-busch.com/anheuser-busch-announces-super-bowl-xlviii-ad-lineup/.

Chapter 1: The Brand Behind the Megaphone

1. Neil deGrasse Tyson, "In the Beginning," Natural History Magazine, September 2003, http://www.haydenplanetarium.org/tyson/read/2003/09/01/in-the-beginning.

2. Edison Research, *The Social Habit* (New Jersey, Edison Research, 2012).

3. Edison Research, *The Infinite Dial* (New Jersey, Edison Research/ Triton Digital, 2015).

4. "Lee Clow on the Art of Media," Media Arts Disruption, accessed July 22, 2015, http://www.mad-blog.com/2010/10/08/lee-clow-on-the-art-of-media/.

5. "brand, n." *OED Online.* Oxford University Press, September 2015, accessed October 19, 2015. http://www.oed.com.

6. "brand," *The American Heritage® Dictionary of the English Language*, 5th edition, accessed October 20, 2015, http://www.yourdictionary.com/brand#americanheritage.

7. Patrick Hanlon, interview by Nick Westergaard, *On Brand* (podcast), Brand Driven Digital, January 1, 2015, http://www.branddrivendigital.com/the-primal-code-of-digital-brand-building-with-patrick-hanlon/.

8. Justin Foster, interview by Nick Westergaard, *On Brand* (podcast), Brand Driven Digital, March 23, 2015, http://www.branddrivendigital.com/why-bacon-brands-beat-oatmeal-brands-with-justin-foster/.

9. "omne trium perfectum," Latin Dictionary, 2008, http://www.latin-dictionary.org, accessed July 22, 2015.

10. Daniel H. Pink, *To Sell Is Human* (New York: Riverhead Books, 2012), 163.

11. Patrick Hanlon, *Primal Branding: Create Zealots for Your Brand, Your Company, and Your Future* (New York: Free Press, 2006), 72–77.

12. Ed Catmull with Amy Wallace, *Creativity, Inc.: Overcoming the Unseen Forces That Stand in the Way of True Inspiration* (New York: Random House, 2014), 86–105.

13. Steve Levigne, interview by Nick Westergaard, *On Brand* (podcast), Brand Driven Digital, May 18, 2015, http://www.branddrivendigital.com/inside-mcdonalds-brand-evolution-with-steve-levigne/.

Chapter 2: Map Your Marketing

1. Lewis Carroll, *Alice's Adventures in Wonderland* (New York: MacMillan, 1865).
2. Rudyard Kipling, *Just So Stories* (New York: Macmillan, 1902).
3. Edison Research, *The Social Habit* (New Jersey, Edison Research, 2012).
4. President John F. Kennedy, speech delivered in person before a joint session of Congress, May 25, 1961.
5. Chip Heath and Dan Heath, *Made to Stick* (New York: Random House, 2007), 95–97.
6. G. T. Doran, "There's a S.M.A.R.T. way to write management's goals and objectives," Management Review (AMA FORUM) 70 (11), 1981, 35–36.
7. Debbie Sterling (CEO, founder of GoldieBlox), in discussion with the author, March 2014.
8. "An in-depth look at the power of viral video: How GoldieBlox tapped 'the holy grail of marketing,'" Bizwomen, The Business Journals, accessed August 4, 2015, http://www.bizjournals.com/bizwomen/news/profiles-strategies/2014/10/how-goldieblox-tapped-the-holy-grail-of-marketing.html.
9. Debbie Sterling, in discussion with the author, March 2014.
10. Heather Whaling (president, Geben Communications), in discussion with the author, March 2014.
11. Kevin Darst (digital manager, New Belgium Brewing), in discussion with the author, October 2015.
12. "Starbucks Celebrates Five-Year Success of My Starbucks Idea," Convenience Store News, accessed August 4, 2015, http://www.csnews.com/starbucks-celebrates-five-year-success-my-starbucks-idea#sthash.LFDAqg8t.dpuf.
13. Jay Baer and Amber Naslund, *The Now Revolution* (New Jersey: John Wiley and Sons), 85.
14. Natalie Brown (owner of Scratch Cupcakery), in discussion with the author, March 2014.

15. "7 Examples of Innovative B2B Content Marketing," Social Media B2B, accessed July 23, 2015, http://socialmediab2b.com/2013/09/7-examples-of-innovative-b2b-content-marketing.

16. Brian Solis, "The Perception Gap: what customers want and what executives think they want [infographic]," accessed July 20, 2015, http://www.briansolis.com/2012/08/the-perception-gap-what-customers-what-and-what-executives-think-they-want/.

Chapter 3: Follow Your Digital Compass

1. *The Edge*. Dir. Lee Tamahori. Perfs. Anthony Hopkins, Alec Baldwin. Fox, 1997. DVD.

2. "Share of Ear™ study shows dramatic increase in podcasting consumption," Edison Research, accessed July 24, 2015, http://www.edisonresearch.com/podcast-share-of-ear/.

3. David Gerhardt (marketing manager, HubSpot), in discussion with the author, August 2015.

4. Edison Research, *The Infinite Dial 2015* (New Jersey: Edison Research, 2015).

5. Edison Research, *The Social Habit* (New Jersey: Edison Research, 2014).

6. TJ Stein (senior director, customer support, Media Temple), in discussion with the author, August 2015.

7. "5 B2C Companies Killing It with Content on LinkedIn," LinkedIn, accessed July 24, 2015, http://marketing.linkedin.com/blog/5-b2c-companies-killing-it-with-content-on-linkedin.

8. Ashley Butler, interview by Nick Westergaard, *On Brand* (podcast), Brand Driven Digital, January 5, 2015, http://www.branddrivendigital.com/the-role-of-brand-voice-in-social-media-at-chobani.

9. "Acura NSX Snapchat Teaser," Shorty Awards, accessed July 24, 2015, http://industry.shortyawards.com/nominee/6th_annual/WU/acura-nsx-snapchat-teaser.

10. Content Marketing Institute/MarketingProfs, *B2B Content Marketing 2015* (Ohio: Content Marketing Institute, 2015).

11. HubSpot, *State of Inbound 2015* (Boston: Hubspot, 2015).

12. Ann Handley and C.C. Chapman, *Content Rules: How to Create Killer Blogs, Podcasts, Videos, Ebooks, Webinars (and More) that Engage Customers and Ignite Your Business* (New Jersey: John Wiley & Sons, 2011), 70.

13. John Jantsch, *The Commitment Engine: Making Work Worth It* (New York: Penguin, 2012), 127.

Chapter 4: Create a Question Engine

1. "Eric Schmidt: Every 2 Days We Create As Much Information As We Did Up To 2003," TechCrunch, accessed July 27, 2015, http://techcrunch.com/2010/08/04/schmidt-data.

2. Google, *Zero Moment of Truth* (Google, 2011).

3. Edison Research, *The Infinite Dial 2015* (New Jersey, Edison Research/Triton Digital, 2015).

4. The Northridge Group, *State of Customer Service Experience 2015* (NRG, 2015).

5. Brian Solis, "The Perception Gap."

6. Daniel Pink, *To Sell Is Human: The Surprising Truth About Moving Others* (New York: Riverhead Books, 2012), 160.

7. Heidi Grant Halvorson (associate director of the Motivation Science Center at Columbia Business School), in discussion with the author, June 2015.

8. Ann Handley and C.C. Chapman, *Content Rules*, 70.

9. "A Revolutionary Marketing Strategy: Answer Customers' Questions," *The New York Times*, accessed July 27, 2015, http://www.nytimes.com/2013/02/28/business/smallbusiness/increasing-sales-by-answering-customers-questions.html.

10. "How River Pools Made $2.5 Million in Sales from a Single Article [Case Study]," Business 2 Community, accessed August 5, 2015, http://www.business2community.com/content-marketing/river-pools-made-2-5-million-sales-single-article-case-study-01131193.

11. Dave Kerpen, *Likeable Social Media: How to Delight Your Customers, Create an Irresistible Brand, and Be Generally Amazing on Facebook (and Other Social Networks)* (New York: McGraw-Hill, 2011), 122.

12. Carie Lewis Carlson (deputy director of online communications, the Humane Society), in discussion with the author, March 2014.

Chapter 5: Embrace Your Power People

1. Samantha Hersil, in discussion with the author, April 2015.
2. Jay Baer, *Youtility: Why Smart Marketing Is About Help Not Hype* (New York: Portfolio, 2013), 150.
3. Content Marketing Institute/MarketingProfs, *B2B Content Marketing 2015* (Ohio: Content Marketing Institute, 2015).
4. Salesforce Marketing Cloud, *2015 State of Marketing* (Salesforce, 2015).
5. Mitch Joel, *Ctrl Alt Delete: Reboot Your Business. Reboot Your Life, Your Future Depends on It* (New York: Hachette Book Group, 2013).
6. Altimeter Group, *Career Path of the Corporate Social Strategist* (Altimeter Group, 2010).
7. Community Management Roundtable, *The State of Community Management* (Community Management Roundtable, 2012).
8. Altimeter Group, *Career Path of the Corporate Social Strategist* (Altimeter Group, 2010).
9. Altimeter Group, *2015 State of Social Business* (Altimeter Group, 2015).
10. "The Scoop on Ben & Jerry's Social Media (Interview)," Brand Driven Digital, accessed January 26, 2012, http://www.branddrivendigital .com/the-scoop-on-ben-jerrys-social-media-interview.
11. Reid Travis (director of marketing communications, Pancheros), in discussion with the author, July 2012.
12. Kevin Darst, in discussion with the author, October 2015.
13. "Inherited Outdoors, Halley Roberts, Santa Fe, NM," Patagonia Worn Wear blog, accessed August 6, 2015, http://wornwear.patagonia.com/ post/74315065037/inherited-outdoors-halley-roberts-santa-fe-nm.
14. Edison Research, *The Social Habit* (New Jersey, Edison Research, 2012).
15. Tamsen Webster (senior vice president for executive communications

and chief marketing officer at Oratium), in discussion with the author, August 2015.

16. Awareness Hub, *State of Social Media Marketing* (Awareness, 2012).

17. "Employees on Facebook are a bright spot in UPS's holiday delivery debacle," Holtz, accessed August 6, 2015, http://holtz.com/blog/facebook/employees-on-facebook-are-a-bright-spot-in-upss-holiday-delivery-debacle/4262.

18. Mark W. Schaefer, interview by Nick Westergaard, *On Brand* (podcast), Brand Driven Digital, April 27, 2015, http://www.brand drivendigital.com/cracking-the-content-code-with-mark-w-schaefer.

Chapter 6: Connect Your Digital Dots

1. Altimeter Group, *2015 State of Social Business* (Altimeter Group, 2015); CMO Survey, *The CMO Survey* (World Market Watch LLC, 2015).

2. "Why Are Marketers Ashamed of Email Marketing," Brand Driven Digital, accessed July 28, 2015, http://www.branddrivendigital.com/why-are-marketers-ashamed-of-email-marketing.

3. MailerMailer, *Email Marketing Metrics Report* (MailerMailer LLC, 2014).

4. ExactTarget, *2012 Channel Preferences Survey* (ExactTarget, 2012).

5. "Email Marketing: How to Push Send and Grow Your Business," Copyblogger, accessed August 6, 2015, http://www.copyblogger.com/email-marketing.

6. eConsultancy, *Email Marketing Industry Census 2012* (eConsultancy, 2012).

7. StrongView, *2015 Marketing Trends Survey* (StrongView Systems Inc, 2015).

8. Ipsos, *Socialogue: Text Me, Text Me Not* (Ipsos Global, 2012).

9. "Why Are Marketers Ashamed of Email Marketing," Brand Driven Digital, accessed July 28, 2015, http://www.branddrivendigital.com/why-are-marketers-ashamed-of-email-marketing.

10. "Businesses That Use Email Marketing and Social Media Achieve

28% Higher Email Open Rates, According to VerticalResponse User Data," accessed July 28, 2015, http://www.verticalresponse.com/about/press/businesses-that-use-email-marketing-and-social-media-achieve-higher-email-open-rates.

11. comScore, *2012 US Digital Future In Focus* (comScore, 2012).

12. StrongView, *2015 Marketing Trends Survey* (StrongView Systems Inc, 2015).

13. Rob Yoegel (former content marketing director, Monetate), in discussion with the author, March 2014.

14. Daniel Rowles, interview by Nick Westergaard, *On Brand* (podcast), Brand Driven Digital, February 28, 2015, http://www.branddrivendigital.com/why-branding-is-the-sum-of-your-digital-touchpoints-with-daniel-rowles.

Chapter 7: The Simplification Game

1. David Srere, interview by Nick Westergaard, *On Brand* (podcast), Brand Driven Digital, April 6, 2015, http://www.branddrivendigital.com/branding-with-simplicity-at-siegelgale.

2. Jay Baer, *Youtility*, p. 146.

3. Content Marketing Institute/MarketingProfs, *B2B Content Marketing 2015* (Ohio: Content Marketing Institute, 2015).

4. Ibid.

5. Ibid.

6. Ibid.

7. Google, *Zero Moment of Truth* (Google, 2011).

8. Ann Handley and C.C. Chapman, *Content Rules*, 66.

9. Mike Hayes (digital marketing manager, Ben and Jerry's), in discussion with the author, January 2013.

10. "Content Shock," Businesses Grow, accessed July 28, 2015, http://www.businessesgrow.com/2014/01/06/content-shock.

11. Content Marketing Institute/MarketingProfs, *B2B Content Marketing 2015* (Ohio: Content Marketing Institute, 2015).

12. Bryan Kramer, interview by Nick Westergaard, *On Brand* (pod-

cast), Brand Driven Digital, February 9, 2015, http://www.brand drivendigital.com/the-art-of-personal-branding-with-bryan-kramer.

13. Edison Research, *The Social Habit* (New Jersey, Edison Research, 2014).

14. Dave Kerpen, *Likeable Social Media*, 77–78.

15. Katie Merritt (communications coordinator, Palmer College of Chiropractic), in discussion with the author, August 2013.

16. Reid Travis (director of marketing communications, Pancheros), in discussion with the author, July 2012.

17. Brian Solis, "The Perception Gap."

Chapter 8: Measure What Matters

1. "ANA Survey Reveals 'Accountability' is the Top Concern for Senior Marketers," Association of National Advertisers, accessed July 29, 2015, http://www.ana.net/content/show/id/25159.

2. Altimeter Group, *Career Path of the Corporate Social Strategist* (Altimeter Group, 2010).

3. "Google Analytics Market Share," Metric Mail, accessed August 7, 2015, http://metricmail.tumblr.com/post/904126172/google-analytics-market-share.

4. Jason Falls (senior vice president of digital strategy, Elasticity), in discussion with the author, March 2014.

5. Altimeter Group, *Career Path of the Corporate Social Strategist* (Altimeter Group, 2010).

6. Natalie Brown (owner, Scratch Cupcakery), in discussion with the author, March 2014.

7. Mark W. Schaefer (author, *Return on Influence*), in discussion with the author, March 2014.

8. Ibid.

9. Altimeter Group, *Career Path of the Corporate Social Strategist* (Altimeter Group, 2010).

10. "Ford CMO Jim Farley: Social media leading to 'massive cost savings' for Ford," MackCollier.com, accessed July 31, 2015, http://

mackcollier.com/ford-cmo-jim-farley-social-media-leading-to-massive-cost-savings-for-ford.

11. Peter Bergen (retired Troll Communications CEO, marketing consultant), in discussion with the author, July 2015.

Chapter 9: Putting It Together

1. Stephen Sondheim, "Putting It Together." *Sunday in the Park with George* (Original Broadway Cast Recording). RCA, 1984. CD.
2. Ipsos, *Socialogue: Text Me, Text Me Not* (Ipsos Global, 2012).
3. Scott Monty (former global head of social media, Ford Motor Company), in discussion with the author, July 2015.
4. "Summit 2013 Highlights: Inciting a B-to-B Content Revolution," SiriusDecisions, accessed July 29, 2015, https://www.siriusdecisions. com/Blog/2013/May/Summit-2013-Highlights-Inciting-a-BtoB-Content-Revolution.aspx.
5. "Content Shock," Businesses Grow, accessed July 28, 2015, http://www.businessesgrow.com/2014/01/06/content-shock.
6. Tim Hayden and Tom Webster, *The Mobile Commerce Revolution: Business Success in a Wireless World* (Indianapolis, Indiana: Que Biz-Tech, 2014).
7. "scrappy." Urban Dictionary. 2008, accessed July 21, 2015, http://www.urbandictionary.com.

ACKNOWLEDGEMENTS

Writing a book is a team effort at every stage. *Get Scrappy* was no exception.

In the fall of 2013, it was Ann Handley and the team at MarketingProfs that first allowed me to explore the scrappy concept at their B2B Forum in Boston. A business author couldn't ask for more helpful mentors than Ann and Jay Baer, of Convince and Convert. As I got my ducks in a row, both were there for me, answering every email throughout the process with thoughtful concern and care.

Speaking of mentors, I can't forget Dorie Clark, who—in addition to being a scrappy marketer herself—has an incredible knack for putting people together. Through a serendipitous dinner she organized at SXSW, I met Heidi Grant Halvorson, who in turn introduced me to my amazing literary agent, Giles Anderson.

Scrappy is an abstract concept to some. I am thankful that Giles believed in this book going out of the gate and was able to connect me with a publisher that understood and was equally excited as well. During our first call, I knew I'd hit it off with AMACOM's Ellen Kadin when she said, "Scrappy—we love that approach." I'd be lost and confused without Erika Spelman, a font of wisdom on everything from permissions to endnote style. Debbie Posner's resourcefulness and wit made editing a breeze. Bradley Dicharry who designed the book cover (as well as all of my logos and websites through the years) always seems to know exactly what my brand should look like. And, of course, everyone who kept encouraging me to include my drawings in the book—you kept me from chickening out on many occasions. Thank you all for helping me bring this concept from the stage to the page.

Thanks also to my proofing team, who took a pass through an early draft of this book. Kristina Paider helped me find my voice and sharpen concepts. My old friend, fellow *Star Trek* fan, and academic colleague Rob Rouwenhorst made sure my i's were dotted, my t's were crossed, and my research was rigorous. And, of course, my mom Linda Westergaard, who has read all of my work through the years, including the early self-published 1987 novelization of the TV show *ALF*. In addition to numerous editorial insights here, she noted (with a smiley face as only an elementary school teacher can) where I accidentally replaced "popped" with "pooped."

And finally, I'm especially thankful for those who really made it possible for me to do this. First, our team at Brand Driven Digital is nothing if not scrappy. From our employees to our community of blog contributors, thank you for keeping our small business afloat during this process. Speaking of business, everything in this book is built on the foundation of the work I'm grateful to do every day with my business partner and father, Dean Westergaard. Thank you for teaching me so much about work, life, and everything in between.

And, of course, I wouldn't know a thing about being scrappy if it wasn't for the fact that I home office with five kids in the house. However, you couldn't ask for a more creative, energetic, and inspiring group of coworkers and collaborators. Thanks Harry, Sam, Adrien, Mia, and Jude for letting me sit across the hall from your toy room and write this.

While others have come and gone throughout this process, Meghann Foster was there for every step, in every way possible. As a sounding board for ideas, a therapist when things weren't going quite right, a professional colleague picking up slack in our work, and a great mom to the aforementioned five kids, her often unseen support is invaluable. As the dedication at the beginning of this book notes, she is, without a doubt, the scrappiest person I know. Thanks for being in my corner.

INDEX

▬ ▬ ▬

ABOUT THE AUTHOR

Nick Westergaard is a strategist, speaker, author, and educator. As chief brand strategist at Brand Driven Digital, he helps build better brands at organizations of all sizes—from small businesses to Fortune 500 companies to the President's Jobs Council.

Since 2005 Nick has written about marketing, posting fresh brand-driven insights each week at branddrivendigital.com. He also writes for MarketingProfs and *The Gazette*, where he is a regular columnist. His thoughts have been featured in news sources such as *US News & World Report*, *Entrepreneur* magazine, Mashable, American Express OPEN Forum, and more. He's also the host of the popular On Brand podcast.

Nick is a sought-after keynote speaker on branding and digital marketing at conferences and corporate events throughout the world. He also organizes and hosts the Social Brand Forum, a premier digital marketing event in the heart of the heartland (Iowa City). Nick teaches at the University of Iowa, where he sits on the Advisory Council of the Marketing Institute at the Tippie College of Business and the Professional Advisory Board for the School of Journalism and Mass Communication. He is also a mentor at the Iowa Startup Accelerator.

Nick lives with his wife and five kids in Coralville, Iowa.

Find him online at nickwestergaard.com and @nickwestergaard on Twitter.